Skills for New Managers

Other titles in the Briefcase Books series include:

To learn more about titles in the Briefcase Books series go to
www.briefcasebooks.com

Skills for New Managers

Second Edition

Morey Stettner

New York Chicago San Francisco Athens
London Madrid Mexico City Milan
New Delhi Singapore Sydney Toronto

1 2 3 4 5 6 7 8 9 0 QFR/QFR 1 8 7 6 5 4 3

ISBN   978-0-07-182714-0
MHID   0-07-182714-5

e-ISBN   978-0-07-182715-7
e-MHID   0-07-182715-3

This is a CWL Publishing Enterprises book developed for McGraw-Hill by CWL Publishing Enterprises, Inc., Madison, Wisconsin, www.cwlpub.com.

Library of Congress Cataloging-in-Publication Data
Stettner, Morey.
  Skills for new managers / Morey Stettner.
    pages   cm
  Revised edition of Skills for new managers, published in 2000.
  Includes index.
    ISBN 978-0-07-182714-0 (alk. paper) — ISBN 0-07-182714-5 (alk. paper) 1. Leadership. 2. Employee motivation. 3. Management. I. Title.
  HD57.7.S736 2014
  658.4--dc23

                                    2013032866

McGraw-Hill Education products are available at special quantity discounts to use as premiums and sales promotions, or for use in corporate training programs. To contact a representative, please visit the Contact Us pages at mhprofessional.com.

This book is printed on acid-free paper.

Contents

Introduction

There's an old joke that generations of disgruntled employees like to tell each other.

"You know what the definition of manager is, don't you?"

"No, tell me."

"A manager is the person who sees the visitors so that everyone else can get the work done."

Maybe that's funny to worker bees. But now that you're a manager, it's your job to laugh *with* your staff, rather than having them laugh *at* you.

There are thousands of managers out there, all trying to recruit, train, and motivate their staff. They all want the same thing: to please their bosses, to earn the respect of their employees, and, above all, to avoid the headaches that so often come with people management.

As a new manager, you may find the whole task daunting. In your old job, you could excel by mastering a specialty. You showed up every day, carved out an area of expertise, and thrived by performing at a level that impressed higher-ups at your organization.

Now you've earned a reward: a staff to manage. From now on, your success no longer depends on your technical abilities and specialized knowledge. You will prosper only if other people do their jobs well. And if they fail, you'll pay the price.

The best managers embrace the challenge with gusto. They build trust with each employee one day at a time, learning how to woo even the most difficult types of workers to push harder, think differently, and stage experiments that help them produce better results. They set high standards and "walk the talk." When problems arise, they mediate them with poise and fairness. During organizational upheavals and wrenching change, they keep employees informed and provide a rock of stability. When setbacks strike, they do not mope and whine about forces they cannot control; instead, they reassure their staff and redirect everyone's focus on what matters most.

Why Read This Book?

Do you have a mentor who helps you unlock all the secrets of managing? If you do, great. This book will serve as an added resource, a way to cross-check whether the advice you're getting squares with some of the latest views on enlightened management.

If you lack a mentor, then consider this book a friendly substitute. While we can't take your calls when you're confronting an emergency or provide a shoulder to cry on when you're going bonkers at work, we can give you plenty of practical pointers on how to handle a range of situations that you'll no doubt face as a manager.

We won't kid you: effective management requires more than reading this book and nodding with approval when you come across a tip or technique that appeals to you. *You must apply what you read.* By sampling the tools you're about to learn, you can evaluate to what extent they work for you and modify them as needed. People are not mathematical equations, so managing them is a fuzzier and more freeform process than inputting hard data. But as long as you commit to putting into practice what we're about to discuss, we promise your time spent reading this book will pay off.

Overview of the Book

In the first chapter, you'll develop a model of the "perfect manager." This becomes your template for what follows. Once you know what kind of traits, skills, and behaviors will make you manage more effectively, you can mold yourself to excel.

Chapter 2 pierces some of the most prevalent myths of people management. If you're guided by mistaken notions of what it takes to lead employees, then your faulty assumptions can interfere with your better judgment and sabotage your ability to manage.

The purpose of Chapter 3 is to help you hit the ground running. Your first month as a new manager will be traumatic enough without having to confront needless crises. By establishing momentum and taking preventive steps to stamp out problems before they arise, you can gain confidence and impress others with your take-charge leadership.

Chapters 4 and 5 work together to give you pointers to polish your communication skills. We begin with the all-important art of listening, a vastly overlooked skill that every strong manager must possess. You may bring great technical ability and plenty of enthusiasm to your new job, but if you hog the spotlight and interrupt constantly, you doom yourself to mediocrity.

In Chapter 5, we move from listening to talking. Sure, you can bat around buzzwords with the head honcho. But that won't help you shine. You also need to ask intelligent questions and organize your thoughts in a tight, appealing package. Persuasion flows from preparation. When you think before you speak, you can win over almost anyone and turn adversaries into allies.

Chapter 6 examines the mysteries of motivation. Many new managers stumble in their efforts to rally the troops. They assume rah-rah theatrics work best, when in fact the best way to motivate is to observe others and identify what matters most to them.

Chapters 7 and 8 guide you through two of the toughest aspects of management: giving criticism and doling out discipline. You probably dread both of these tasks. But if you learn to do them well, you can proceed with the knowledge that you're a fair-minded, respected manager.

The key to criticizing employees is helping them realize for themselves how their performance can improve. By steering clear of harsh generalizations and, instead, describing a specific activity in neutral terms, you remove personality from the equation and increase the odds your criticism will pay off.

When disciplining, you'll learn how and when to "write up" an employee. Timing counts. If you rush to accuse or lash out, you can turn into a tyrant. But if you wave a wet noodle rather than whip poor performers into shape, you can wind up managing a losing team.

Chapter 9 gives you the tools to organize yourself. Many new managers trip themselves up by losing track of time and getting buried in minutiae. By tracking your work and avoiding time-killing tasks, you can boost your productivity and squeeze the most out of every hour.

Every manager must delegate, and that's the subject of Chapter 10. It's easy to bark orders and await results. But your style of giving directions will largely determine whether your employees comply or rebel.

Chapter 11 focuses on managing your boss rather than your workers. Keeping higher-ups apprised of your progress and maintaining open lines of communication can eliminate misunderstandings and ensure that you get the credit you deserve for your efforts.

In Chapter 12, we show you how to capitalize on your new role as manager to climb the ladder. That involves networking. The wider your web of contacts both inside and outside your organization, the faster you can nab promotions or pounce on career opportunities.

Chapter 13 explores team leadership. You'll learn how to extract the most value from teams, recruit the right players, and focus everyone's efforts on what matters most. If you're a fan of group brainstorming sessions, you'll learn about recent research that exposes the limits of gathering people in a room and encouraging them to "go wild" with crazy ideas.

Finally, in Chapter 14, you'll confront five tests that every new manager must face. These are tough challenges that require shrewd judgment and attention to detail. Clear these five critical hurdles, and you'll be well on your way to excelling in your new role.

Special Features

The idea behind the books in the Briefcase Series is to give you practical information written in a friendly, person-to-person style. The chapters are short, deal with tactical issues, and include lots of examples. They also feature numerous sidebars designed to give you different types of specific information. Here's a description of the boxes you'll find in this book.

KEY TERM

Every subject has some jargon, including this one, dealing with management. These sidebars provide definitions of terms and concepts as they are introduced.

SMART

MANAGING

These sidebars do just what their name suggests: give you tips and tactics for using the ideas in this book to intelligently manage through the use of effective management practices and smart principles of human interaction.

TRICKS OF THE TRADE

Tricks of the Trade sidebars give you insider how-to hints on techniques new managers can use to execute the tactics described in this book.

FOR EXAMPLE

It's always useful to have examples that show how the principles in the book are applied. These sidebars provide descriptions of on-the-job situations illustrating how successful managers handle different situations.

CAUTION

Caution sidebars provide warnings for where things could go wrong when dealing with employees so you can avoid the landmines that frequently plague new managers.

MISTAKE PROOFING

How can you make sure you won't make a mistake when you're trying to implement the techniques the book describes? You can't, but these sidebars give you practical advice on how to minimize the possibility of things going wrong.

This icon identifies sidebars where you'll find specific procedures, techniques, or technology you can use to successfully implement the book's principles and practices.

TOOLS

Skills for New Managers

The Perfect New Manager

R andy's dream has come true. An insurance underwriter for the last four years, he can finally call himself a manager. His boss recently told him, "You've worked hard, the agents like you, and your results have been outstanding. So we're going to put you in charge of one of our underwriting units. Our hope is you'll teach your employees how you do it, and your success will rub off on them."

Just like that, 10 employees now report to Randy. He walks into his new office (a real office, not a cubicle!) and looks around in a daze. He has wanted to manage a staff ever since he visited his division head's huge home many years ago and noticed how well a "boss" could live. And he figures that once he proves that he can handle a group of crusty, cynical underwriters and help them boost their results, the sky's the limit for him.

Who's Your Model?

Like so many new managers, Randy assumes that he can do the job better than others who've come before him because he realizes what mistakes not to make. He's had seven bosses in his career, and he knows exactly what they did right and wrong. The same thing happens when proud parents hold their newborn and declare confidently to each other, "Let's raise this adorable baby the right way, not like our parents did it!"

You may think you know what it takes to manage well. After all, you're an earnest straight shooter who gets along well with a wide range of people. You like challenges and you dread boring routines. Experienced managers have told you that "every day is different" when you're in charge of a staff, and that sounds just fine with you.

But the real test of your management skills rests on your ability to grow into the job. No newly minted manager can possibly anticipate what it's like to direct people. Each day brings weird scenarios you could never predict, from the clerk who bursts into tears for no apparent reason (what do you do?) to the disgruntled veteran who issues a veiled threat against you and your company.

There's no way this or any book can show you how to respond to every type of conflict. But we can help you sharpen your natural leadership skills and model yourself after effective managers so that you analyze how *they* would handle a similar situation.

My Favorite Manager

Think of the best boss you ever had. If no one pops to mind, consider a strong leader you know such as a sports coach or a volunteer coordinator at your community center. Complete these

TOOLS sentences:

1. When faced with adversity, this manager will _____.
2. To improve teamwork, this manager will _____.
3. When explaining a concept, this manager will _____.
4. To keep control of an unruly group, this manager will _____.
5. Employees respect this manager because _____.

By imagining how a top-notch manager would manage various scenarios, you give yourself a road map to follow. The individual you admire most serves as your template. Even if you're not sure how this person would deal with specific issues or perform certain tasks, trying to picture such responses can help.

In deciding whom to model, consider your organizational culture. Say you work in a laid-back environment filled with brainy graduate students engaged in medical testing or software programming. In such a setting, you want to promote a calm, cerebral, and creative atmosphere where your employees can operate at their best. Trying to model yourself after a loud, hard-charging executive whom you admire will backfire, because those kind of rah-rah theatrics will fall flat in such an intellectually driven office.

Also confirm how you chose the person whom you seek to emulate. You don't want to select a role model just because she's your best friend or you share certain interests. It's best to model yourself after a manager whom you respect more than like. You want to learn from someone who takes action decisively and exemplifies the kind of behaviors that you think make that individual a superior manager.

Rating Your Leadership

The more you know yourself, the better you'll manage. If you lack a strong sense of self, you'll get manipulated by more forceful personalities who can tell you're a pushover. They'll feed you what you like to hear. And they'll press your hot buttons when they want to rile you.

You need to develop a strong spine to manage. If it hasn't happened yet, the day will come when you'll need to state an unpopular position and stick to it, despite disappointment from employees and even derision from bosses. You'll need to believe in yourself when doubts swirl around you, especially as the stakes mount and the pressure builds. That's when your reserves of poise and confidence will sustain you.

To gain self-awareness, take the following diagnostic tests. Your ratings will help you uncover the strengths and weaknesses that influence how you manage.

TEST 1: PATIENCE

Rate yourself on this 1-to-5 scale:

1. Never
2. Occasionally
3. Sometimes
4. Usually
5. Always

When I tell someone to do something and he or she doesn't do it, I say it again in an angry tone. _____

When someone talks too slowly, I interrupt. _____

When I see someone do something wrong, I instantly point it out. ___

> When someone keeps me waiting more than a minute or two, I resent it.
> _____
>
> When someone doesn't answer my question right away, I cut in and repeat it. _____

Add up your score. If your total is 17 or more, you could stand to lighten up and calm down. You need to relax and cut yourself (and others) some slack. Your lack of patience might reflect an overly controlling mindset, where you steer conversations and direct people more aggressively than is necessary.

If you scored 16 or less, note any 4s or 5s. These indicate areas you can work on that will lower your blood pressure and raise your ability to build trust and gain compliance.

TEST 2: COMMUNICATION SKILLS

Rate yourself on this 1-to-5 scale:

1. Never
2. Occasionally
3. Sometimes
4. Usually
5. Always

When I ask a question, I'm very curious to hear the answer. _____

I like to speak in front of groups. _____

If I disagree, I confirm I've understood the other person before I give my view. _____

If I need to cover many points, I outline what I want to say ahead of time.

_____

When I give instructions or explain complex ideas, I number each item.

_____

If you scored 15 or less, you're probably losing opportunities to bond with others. Your employees can tell if you're distracted or uninterested in what they say, and they won't like it. And if you ramble or hop from topic to topic aimlessly, they're liable to tune out or lose track of your point. Disliking public speaking won't necessarily kill your chances of managing well, but by developing at least some strategies to radiate enthusiasm and arouse the passion of an audience, you can add a valuable weapon to your management arsenal.

TEST 3: ETHICS

Rate yourself on this 1-to-5 scale:

1. Never
2. Occasionally
3. Sometimes
4. Usually
5. Always

I set an example of the high ethical standard I want my staff to follow. _____

If I'm in an ethical bind, I'll talk forthrightly to a wise mentor. _____

I prefer to admit past wrongdoing rather than cover it up and hope I don't get caught. _____

I apply "the sniff test" when confronting an ethical dilemma: if it smells bad, I don't do it. _____

I'm at peace with my ethical behavior. _____

A score of 18 or below should alert you to some questionable attitudes about right and wrong. If your total falls under 15, then you might as well kiss your management career good-bye now rather than wait for the inevitable downfall.

We all make moral decisions every day, whether we realize it or not. If we break rules routinely or grab whatever we can take without a moment's hesitation, then we doom ourselves to alienating the very employees we need to win over. Expedience has its place, but crossing ethical boundaries whenever the situation warrants it weakens your credibility as a leader. Sure, you can probably get away with managing by deception, double-crossing, and denials, but only if you're willing to lose everything in a flash.

Integrity is more than a management tool. It's what enables you to lead by example.

Drafting Your Own "Management Credo"

Earlier in this chapter, you thought about the best boss you ever had. Now it's time to consider the kind of boss *you* want to be.

Developing a *credo*—or set of beliefs—can serve as a constant reminder of what you want to achieve in your new job. This process means more than hashing out detailed, work-related objectives, such as setting projected annual revenues for your unit or maintaining low turnover. It's more lofty than that. You should prepare for the challenges of management by identifying the traits you want to embody and the commitments you're willing to make to yourself to succeed.

To begin, set aside 30 minutes during a calm, unhurried part of the day, perhaps Sunday morning when you're not distracted by workday pressures. Plant yourself in front of your computer—or settle down with pen and paper—and pretend it's a year from now.

Ask yourself, "If I were one of my employees who's been reporting to me for the past year, how do I want to be perceived as a boss?"

Answer this question *from the employee's perspective.* Play the role of one of your direct reports and imagine you're giving yourself a performance review. Address key areas such as communication skills, leadership, reliability, motivational style, and fostering teamwork.

WHAT'S YOUR GRADE?
Glance at an old performance review form that you've received in one of your former jobs. Use the same categories to grade yourself as a boss—from A to F. Be realistic. Imagine you're a fair-minded employee who wants to grade you—the boss—as accurately and objectively as possible.

If you've treated this exercise seriously, you should come away with a revealing self-assessment of your managerial strengths and shortcomings. Armed with this information, you're now ready to compose a management credo.

Here are two examples of real management credos from my clients.

KEY TERM **Management credo** A written set of beliefs that summarizes your goals as a manager and the commitments you're willing to make to get there.

A 25-year-old salesperson who's about to start as sales manager: *I want to lead by example. If my sales team sees that I'm honest, forthright, and dedicated, then they'll strive to act the same. I believe in listening more than talking, and not trying to have all the answers. I will praise well-earned success and support employees who need guidance. I will not accept anything less than a full effort from myself or anyone else.*

A 31-year-old counselor at a nonprofit agency who's about to start as executive director: *I believe in taking responsibility for what I can control and not wasting time with events I cannot control. I will manage others the way I want to be managed: with openness and fairness.*

MY GOALS:

1. *To earn everyone's respect.*
2. *To develop each of my employees to reach a higher potential.*
3. *To push everyone (including me) so that we don't get complacent.*

I COMMIT TO:

1. *Taking bad news well without losing my temper.*
2. *Setting the highest standard of behavior so that there's no confusion over what's the right thing to do.*
3. *Remembering to recognize employees' acts of kindness and selflessness.*
4. *Asking for employees' feedback on my performance regularly rather than losing touch.*

When you draft your management credo, remember that you're not trying to please or impress anyone. It's designed as a private rallying cry, a mission statement that directs your efforts. Write in your own voice and stick to what you believe in most deeply. Probe to uncover *why* you want to manage people in the first place. Your answer should help you compose a credo that you will be more likely to follow.

The length of your final document should range from 50 to 200 words. Don't pad it to lend a false sense of depth. It's better not to waste words or repeat yourself.

Choose a format that works for you. As you see from the above examples, one manager broke it down into "My Goals" and "I Commit to," while the other simply wrote out a few sentences and left it at that. Make a numbered list or use bullet points if that will help you express your thoughts.

> **FAKING IT**   **CAUTION**
>
> Write your management credo in your own words. Don't try to copy a passage that you've read on the Internet or quote from a leader whom you admire. While it's fine to get inspiration from others, every word of the credo should come from within you. It must be an entirely original, heartfelt testament to what you perceive as your fundamental purpose as a manager.

When you've completed this task, put it aside for a few days. Don't even think about it. Then take a fresh look at your management credo. Read it all the way through without judging it or making any changes. Let it sink in for another day. Then and only then should you tweak what you've written—and only if you feel it needs sharpening.

Paying the Price of Success

The perfect new manager knows that perfection doesn't come cheap. Learning to lead a diverse set of employees is a harrowing, confounding, and downright painful process.

You should realize what you're getting into by accepting a people management role, at least in the first few months:

- You may not sleep nearly as well at night.
- You'll bring the job home and possibly take out your frustrations on family and friends.
- You'll find yourself putting out fires, despite your best attempts to prevent personnel crises.
- You'll question your judgment when you delegate a task and then find it wasn't done well.
- You may lose trust in coworkers when you confide in someone and word leaks out, or your "confidential" communication surfaces online as employees blog about you or post your emails.

In short, expect to feel overwhelmed. That's normal. Almost all new managers tell me that they had no idea how consuming management would be. They often report that "the honeymoon period was so short" or "I had no idea what I was getting into." Usually they're not complaining—just stunned.

I'm not trying to drown you in pessimism. Managing people is a blast as long as you understand that it's not a tidy, orderly, predictable business.

TRICKS OF THE TRADE

SUSPEND JUDGMENT
In your first few months as a new manager, don't take things too hard. Avoid chastising yourself for rookie mistakes. Commit to learning at least one lesson from each day, even if you embarrass yourself in the process. Don't insist on judging every decision or magnifying every mishap. Keep your priorities straight and take it one day at a time.

Adaptability, flexibility, and maturity come in handy. So does a dose of good-natured humor that brightens everyone's day.

What's your reward? The best managers often gain more responsibility—fast. More is expected of them, so senior executives tend to raise the bar steadily to see how well these promising supervisors respond to fresh challenges. It can be a heady climb, and the big victories await those who can overcome early obstacles, bear down, and deliver stellar results.

Just because you're not good friends with your employees doesn't mean relationships no longer matter. The opposite is true. The bonds

NO FRIEND OF MINE
MISTAKE PROOFING!

Draw the line between manager and employee now, not later. Don't assume that just because you've worked alongside buddies in the past they'll remain friends. The dynamics of the relationship must change now that you're a manager. It's best that everyone remain cordial and professional, but not so friendly that you play favorites or stir jealousies. Your best bet: find your friends somewhere else.

you establish with your staff serve as the invisible glue that brings everyone together to work toward a common goal.

"Use" Your Employees—Without Making Them Feel Used

New managers sometimes let the rush of authority go to their heads. They suddenly feel awash with entitlement. They start to view themselves as special, different, superior. They may exempt themselves from standard rules of decorum, such as saying "please" or "thank you."

For example, I met a marketing manager, Wes, who was six weeks into his new position. His bosses couldn't understand how Wes had faltered so fast. He had alienated his employees by imposing all kinds of crazy edicts, ranging from an absurdly rigid dress code to having them log their day's work in fifteen-minute increments on elaborate reporting forms that he designed and distributed. The staff was verging on mutiny.

Wes wasn't a villain. He just lost his bearings. As he put it sheepishly to me, "I guess I got carried away by this whole thing. Being in charge brings out another side of me that even I don't always recognize. Sometimes I think my people are tools to be used to get a job done, and I forget they're actually human beings."

I advised Wes to settle down, draft a management credo, and make corrections in his leadership style. Even though his employees saw him as a micromanaging tyrant, the truth was he had lost his confidence and overcompensated by tightening his grip over his staff.

CHECK YOUR EGO

CAUTION

Beware of equating strong, gutsy, aggressive management with suffocating your workers in needless directives. If you indulge your grandiose sense of self-importance, you may come across as an insecure manager who feeds off the attention that you force others to give you. What's worse, by going out of your way to exert your newfound power, you may drive away the very people you'll need to succeed.

Even if you keep your ego under wraps as a new manager, you must still find a way to harness your employees' talents to maximum effect. Put crassly, that means using them to make you look good. The effective manager does this wisely and with their full buy-in, rather than exploiting them shamelessly and then hogging the credit for their hard work.

The best way to use employees is to release everything out into the open. Let them know exactly how they're being used. That's right: Make it clear what you want from them and why their performance matters. These phrases may help:

- *As a result of your work, we will be able to . . .*
- *I'm asking you to make a larger contribution by getting the following work done . . .*
- *Here's a way for us to use your skills more effectively . . .*

By leveling with your staffers, you make *them* feel important (not vice versa). Let them know that you need their best effort, and they'll feel like valuable team members rather than cogs in a wheel.

If you'll benefit from their hard work, don't keep it a secret. Most employees know full well that they can choose whether to make you look like a genius or a goat. Same goes in professional sports, such as a basketball team that gives up on its coach. The players may slack off because they want to get the coach fired—or they may intentionally foil

---

EXPLOIT PRIDE, NOT LABOR
You'll score big wins by getting your employees to push themselves to attain better results. But at the same time, you don't want to turn them into drones who grow over-worked and resentful. Solution: Let them judge themselves. Have them self-administer performance reviews as a prelude to the formal appraisal process where you give your input. Most workers will come down tougher on them-selves than you would, thus allowing you to ally yourself with them (whether you agree with their honest self-evaluation or tell them to lighten up).

---

the coach's plans. If the coach tries to exploit players improperly, the backlash can lead to a humiliating and public termination.

Testing Your Assumptions

Most new managers assume they know exactly what it takes to thrive in their new position. But jumping to such conclusions can lead them astray.

From my experience advising new managers, here are the three most common assumptions they make:

1. The same skills that got me here will help me succeed.
2. Employees expect me to have all the answers.
3. My employees aren't all that different from me.

Let's hold each of these assumptions up to the light and see what we dis-cover.

Assumption 1: Just Do the Same Thing, But Better

Why were you promoted into management? Don't think for a moment your professional expertise instantly qualifies you to lead others. Sure, you may be a math whiz, a social media maven, or a gifted software engi-neer. But whatever accolades you've earned based on your specialized knowledge will in no way guarantee that you'll make a great manager.

In fact, your ability to manage people has almost nothing to do with the technical savvy you've gained that has led you to this point in your career. While you may need to train employees and share your wisdom, the more pressing task ahead is to earn their trust and motivate them to perform exceptionally.

It's scary but true: as a new manager, you're starting from scratch. You cannot fall back on whatever got you this far.

Assumption 2: I Must Have All the Answers

One of the hardest lessons for cub managers to learn is to say "I don't know."

If you think your employees will expect you to know everything, you're wrong. They realize you're just doing your job—and your job is to keep an eye on them. When they ask you questions, they may certainly hope for a satisfying answer. But if you don't supply it, they're not going to mock you behind your back or suspect you're an impostor. They'll probably either forget about it or—if they really want an answer—they'll ask someone else.

No manager knows it all. Ironically, some of the best leaders actually know less than their employees about the innards of the business. This supposed ignorance allows them to bring a much-valued, fresh perspective to the workplace.

The true test of your managing isn't what you know or don't know. It's how you relate to your employees and how you go about helping them find answers.

Assumption 3: I'll Manage Employees Like I Manage Myself

Here's a news flash you'd better process now, not later: your staffers are not reflections of you. They were not made in your image, and they do not embody all the same beliefs, biases, and hopes that you possess.

This may sound obvious. But many managers, flying high on the they're-just-like-me assumption, wind up systematically alienating every one of their employees.

Say you like to play devil's advocate when analyzing an issue. This helps you see both sides before you draw a conclusion. Fair enough.

Yet your employee may not appreciate your thought process. In fact, she may view your critical response to her idea as a thinly veiled rejection. She may think *you really believe that*—that you don't want to give her proposal serious consideration. She won't see it as harmless devil's advocacy; she'll walk away convinced that you just love to knock employees' good ideas, and she may spread the word among her coworkers.

Perhaps you've established a solid track record as a technician. Great. But most of those skills won't necessarily help you handle others. That's an eye-opener for many hotshots who are promoted into management. They figure that they're unstoppable, only to find that all their specialized training doesn't matter much when they go face-to-face with their staff.

If you must make an assumption, here's a safe one: your employees are all different. They can listen to the same speech and hear different messages. What frightens you might excite them, and what motivates you might bore them.

Acknowledge the diversity among your team. Don't project onto others as you see yourself. The more you can treat each individual separately, the more you'll grow to marvel at the wide range of attitudes and behaviors that your employees bring to work every day.

New Manager's Checklist for Chapter 1

☑ Model yourself after star managers. Analyze the keys to their success, and use this as your template.

☑ Gain confidence by becoming more aware—but less judgmental—of how you manage others.

☑ Write a management credo that lists the traits you want to embody and the commitments you're willing to make to succeed.

☑ Expect to be overwhelmed as a new manager. Prepare to pay an early price for success.

☑ Exploit your employees' pride, not their labor. It's fine to use them for your own self-gain as long as you satisfy their own interests, too.

☑ Avoid assumptions that block your ability to manage your employees.

Piercing Six Myths of Management

As soon as she heard, Sandra called her husband with the great news. "I've just been promoted," she said. "I've been named manager of the data processing unit!"

Almost immediately, she began to think out loud about how she'd manage. "I'm going to be friends with everyone. I'm going to decide stuff quickly, not dilly-dally over every little thing. I'll run a tight ship and restore order, and I'll stand by my people the way a leader should. Most of all, I'm not taking any guff from anyone. They'll know that what I say goes."

While Sandra clearly wants to do well, her comments raise a few red flags. She will soon discover that, while her views of management certainly sound reasonable, they won't prove all that workable in the real world.

Sandra's not alone. Misconceptions abound when it comes to managing people properly. These false beliefs can befuddle even the most well-intentioned leaders who want to start out on the right foot.

Most new supervisors want it all. They may try to treat their employees as friends while never looking weak or admitting error. They may proudly side with their workers even as they make rash decisions that ignore their staff's concerns. They may order people around without listening, under the impression that leaders must charge ahead without hesitation.

Sandra's not doomed to fail. If she's smart, she will realize in due time that her idealism won't cut it. Experience will teach her to separate the myths from the reality of effective people management.

Myth 1: You Must Call *All* the Shots

Employees make an average of 100 unsupervised decisions a day. No matter how much power you think you possess as manager, you cannot possibly insert yourself into every situation and play the king or queen.

Don't believe for a second that just because you're a manager, you're in charge of everything. The fact that you're the boss gives you the right to delegate, to enable others to call the shots on your behalf. By pulling back and putting employees in the driver's seat, you can lead quietly and spread the authority. That's how to build loyalty and teamwork.

According to recent research by Towers Watson, a global consulting firm, managers that give employees more autonomy in deciding how, when, and where they perform their work raise the collective engagement level. When you allow people to think for themselves and make their own judgment calls, you'll find that they're more vested in successful outcomes.

COLLABORATION IN ACTION

FOR EXAMPLE When Mike took over as manager, he introduced himself to his employees in a meeting and listed five key staffing decisions he had to make right away. Rather than telegraph his answers or insist that he would study the issues thoroughly and make the right calls, Mike did something unusual: he asked the group to select representatives who could advise him on each of the five areas he needed to evaluate. Thus, the group chose its own panel of experts whom Mike could turn to for input. Thanks to these employee advisors, Mike collaborated with them to make smart decisions.

The irony of this myth is that no manager in his right mind would want to call all the shots. That's a surefire way to a rapid flameout. Viewed strictly in terms of energy saving, you would exhaust yourself if you took it upon yourself to make every decision.

Another danger is that you may suffocate your employees. You cannot achieve any collective triumph if you're always at the wheel, never allowing anyone else to steer. If you treat employees like gophers, they'll begin to think like gophers. And you'll be all alone, carrying the weight of the world—or at least all the problems that come with your job.

Let's look at how this myth can creep up on an unsuspecting new manager. Say you've just taken over a back-office operation with a dozen employees. You figure that in order to assert your leadership, you need to dive right into the job rather than sit back and wait for crises to arise. So you spend a few days processing customer orders alongside your lowest-level clerks.

So far, so good. You show your staff you're not too proud to roll up your sleeves and do some grunt work.

But you don't stop there. During your first day in the trenches, you point out what you perceive as inefficiencies.

You say, "Hold on. I don't think you need to fill out every field on every computer screen." Then you turn to another clerk and say, "You keep getting error messages because you're rushing too much and entering the wrong information. You need to slow down and type everything correctly the first time."

You're meddling without even realizing it, calling all the shots when there's no need to say a word. You're not trying to be a pest; in fact, you think that you're actually making their job *easier*.

But they grumble at your suggestions. They have their reasons for operating the way they do. Perhaps they've discovered that they save time in the long run by completing every field because the system stalls otherwise. But a meek employee may not feel comfortable telling you this key piece of information. And even though you observed someone else getting a string of error messages, that person may have known the reason for those error prompts had nothing to do with typos. Some automated systems have their quirks—and experienced users

WHEN TO LAY OFF

Before you give an order, ask yourself two questions, "What will happen if I wait another week and see what happens?" and "Do I have all the facts I need?" If you keep quiet, maybe your employee can fix what's broken without your involvement. By observing more closely, you may also discover that your order either wasn't necessary or would actually make matters worse.

get accustomed to such quirks and proceed in what they deem the fastest, most efficient manner.

Myth 2: You Can't Trust Anyone

Before Julia agreed to become a manager, she sought advice from a grizzled veteran at her firm. When she asked him if she should take the job, he said, "It depends. You're awfully trusting, and that'll get you into trouble. I never trusted my staff. If you blindly trust people, you'll fail."

Julia couldn't believe what she was hearing. She always thought that managers had to trust their employees, at least to some degree. As a trusting soul, she never imagined that would work against her. She didn't think of herself as naive, just willing to give most people the benefit of the doubt.

In fact, Julia's colleague was perpetuating a destructive management myth. Many managers who embrace the traditional command-and-control model believe that it's foolish to trust employees. The thinking goes, "If I assume every employee is up to no good, I won't be taken advantage of. And if I install enough checks and balances in the system, I can catch wrongdoers quickly and get rid of them."

A corollary of this myth is the mistaken belief that managers must always put themselves first—over the organization's needs and their employees' best interests. Because they've heard that "it's lonely at the top," new managers may decide to install web monitoring software on employees' company-owned computers to spy on their workers and plant gossip that helps them pull the levers in the rumor mill.

I've found a surprising number of rookie managers buy into this myth. Many outwardly warm, friendly professionals carry a cauldron of distrust inside of them, and they actually believe such paranoia will serve them well as managers. In all fairness, however, they know we live in a litigious society. They hear about outrageous lawsuits filed by employees who claim various sorts of discrimination, harassment, and wrongful discharge. They want to keep their guard up, and that vigilance chips away at their willingness to trust.

Refusing to trust anyone won't help you manage more effectively, and you'll certainly isolate yourself. But blind trust is equally dangerous. You need to let your relationships with your employees evolve naturally, realizing that some stumbles will occur along the way. Not everyone can keep a secret, but that doesn't mean you must paint all your workers as loose-lipped blabbermouths. And now more than ever, some new hires will profess loyalty only to quit when they get a better offer elsewhere. As a manager, you'll learn that trust flows both ways.

GIVE TRUST A CHANCE　　**SMART**

Here's how to give employees a chance to earn your trust. Call a staffer into your office and close the door. Say, "I'd **MANAGING** like you to keep what I'm about to tell you confidential." Then share a few harmless, noncontroversial bits of news that you reveal to no one else. Wait a few weeks and monitor the grapevine. If word spreads, at least you know whom *not* to trust. While this isn't a foolproof test, it's a good starting point to screen employees.

Myth 3: You Must Remain Objective at All Times

During World War II, many Americans idolized the dry-eyed, stone-faced foreign correspondents who reported from Europe. They were seen as gutsy, tough-as-nails journalists who could keep their composure amid the brutal fighting and bloody bombing runs.

Today, many new managers buy into the same myth. Like a would-be Edward R. Murrow, the famed World War II newsman, the typical supervisor may try to come across as a steely, expressionless fighter who's unfazed by the craziness that surrounds him.

As much as you may want to act like a cool-under-fire leader, too much coolness can strip away your natural personality. There's no rule that requires managers to act like robots, bouncing from task to task without showing any trace of emotion. In fact, your eagerness to play the part of *Star Trek*'s Mr. Spock—all calm and rational—can backfire. You'll lose countless opportunities to connect with your team and to inspire them to reach greater heights.

In your first few months as manager, you may go out of your way to sound serious. You may hold in your laugh or refuse to crack a joke to enliven a discussion. You may greet an employee's enthusiasm with stony silence, thinking that it would be immature or imprudent to get carried away. When someone looks shaken or cries in your presence, you may offer some tissues stoically and pretend it doesn't affect you in the least.

Beware: this android-like behavior won't help you manage people any better. You want to appear strong and resilient, but you'll appear heartless and detached. You want to set an example of hardened determination, but you'll come across as a manager blinded by tunnel vision and unable to empathize with others.

> ### SOUND LIKE YOU MEAN IT
>
> Your communication style at work should not differ all that much from the way you chat with friends and family. Here's how to make sure you're not lapsing into an emotionless monotone: Tape yourself the next time you give a presentation or lead a staff meeting. Play back your tape to a good friend who knows you outside of work. Ask if you sound any different. Ideally, your friend should recognize your workplace personality as consistent with how you sound at other times.

There's a time and a place for remaining objective, of course, as long as you don't overdo it. If you're shifting into data-gathering mode, you'll want to collect information dispassionately without judging it. This can occur when you investigate an employee's complaint, experiment with different solutions to a thorny problem, or analyze results from customer surveys.

Similarly, when you must say no to an employee, base your answer on facts rather than emotions. You'll find it easier to muster the courage to come down hard if you've aligned plenty of concrete evidence to support your position. You can reinforce your firm no-means-no answer by sticking to hard data—without allowing your emotions to surface. Losing your hard-nosed objectivity can prolong the decision-making process. Employees can sense that you're subject to an emotional appeal, and they may repeat their requests while tugging at your heartstrings.

Myth 4: You Must Defend Your Staff

Ron's boss didn't sound happy. She summoned him into her office, closed the door, and started to chastise him for his lackadaisical supervision of his customer service staff.

"Your people don't even answer the phone on the fourth ring," she said. "And when they finally say hello, they sound bored and listless. I even heard one of them sigh—loudly—into the phone. I felt like I was being a pest, when all I was doing was asking for help. You've got to do a better job training these people and watching them to make sure they perform up to our standards."

Ron instinctively did what he thought he had to do: defend his staff. He excused them for sounding harassed, but they're "overworked because we're short staffed." He explained that many customers who ask for help hang up in frustration because they lack the patience to listen to step-by-step solutions, so his employees "understandably dread this task." He said that with the air-conditioning broken, his customer service reps were hot and irritable over the last week, which contributed to their phone manner.

Regardless of what you think of Ron's points, you should realize by now that he did not have to stand up for his employees' poor performance. His boss wasn't asking for excuses or explanations; she wanted the problem fixed, period. Ron's insistence on defending his staff only made her angrier and lowered her estimation of Ron's managerial ability.

TALK LESS, EXTRACT MORE

TRICKS OF THE TRADE

The next time you're tempted to defend your staff from a boss's or colleague's attack, try this strategy: Listen without interrupting. Wait patiently for the speaker to unload all of his concerns or criticisms about your employees. Don't rush to respond; instead, pose a few follow-up questions to gather more information. Or simply ask for examples. The advantage of this is twofold: you avoid falling into the trap of providing an instant defense *and* you show you're the kind of mature manager who can face unwelcome news head-on and dig for additional facts.

You can tell that you're clinging to this myth if you start to take any criticism of your staff personally. You may react impulsively to any hint that they're not pulling their weight. In extreme cases, you may lose perspective and glorify your employees as unsung heroes who can do no wrong.

A big part of managing others is learning to separate your own performance from theirs. If they let you down or prove ineffectual despite your efforts to train them, that's life. Your employees may fail, and your bosses may not like what they see. That's unavoidable, so prepare for it. Mount a defense only when you're sure it's justified.

It's fine to stick up for people who are unfairly accused or judged harshly by others in the organization who lack accurate information. But you should never grow so attached to your team that you rush to defend their every move without first assessing the merits of what you hear.

Myth 5: You Cannot Back Down

If you grew up having to fend off bullies, perhaps you learned one of the harsh lessons of the school yard: the only way to win a brawl is to remain the last one standing. Backing down equals humiliation.

Thankfully, the same rules don't apply in the workplace. In fact, the ability to stay out of fights and give up ground to a more forceful opponent is sometimes your smartest move. But some fresh-faced managers may recall their days on the playground, when taking punch after punch was better than walking away, leading them to conclude that they must never, ever give an inch.

I find many supervisors mistakenly think that once they stake out a position, they must prove that they're right at all costs. Or they may go out of their way to prove that they're in charge by refusing to apologize, admit error, or revisit an issue that they've already attempted to resolve. It's a myth that they seem to embrace enthusiastically because it gives them a sense of power and infallibility. Even if their conscience tells them to reverse course, they can rest easy knowing that as the boss, they're supposed to take a firm stand and not budge.

Here are six situations when you have more to gain by disregarding this misleading myth and backing down rather than playing the role of a stubborn fighter:

1. **You state the wrong facts.** When you base a decision on incorrect information, there's nothing to gain by clinging to your conclusion. Your staff won't lose any respect for you if you acknowledge the truth in a forthright manner. Even if you've already given orders that you now must withdraw or modify, it's better to do that than to keep quiet and let the damage spread.

2. **You're fighting for peanuts.** If you're negotiating a million-dollar contract, it's obviously unwise to backpedal at the first sign of resistance. But if a conflict erupts over how you intend to punish an employee for an unexcused 30-minute absence during an otherwise quiet day, then you're going to squander precious goodwill to "win" a minor skirmish. Other employees will take notice and view your every move with suspicion.

3. **Circumstances change.** New managers should stand their ground when they want to prove a point and showcase their leadership. But if events unfold unpredictably and it's no longer worth fighting the battle, then it's silly to withstand the forces of change. Example: You don't want to back down after putting an employee on probation for violating the dress code, despite protestations from other workers. But then your company's president announces a new policy: every day is now casual day with looser guidelines regarding clothing. Now you have a convenient "out," so take it.

4. **Precedent saves you.** If other managers in your organization have backed down when faced with a similar challenge—and survived to tell about it—then you're safe following their lead. This often happens when an incoming manager tries to enact stricter forms of discipline, only to unleash a staff rebellion. Then the news spreads that another manager who tried the same tough strategy wound up compromising with employees over what types of discipline would ultimately apply. You can save face by telling your employee, "I'm willing to be flexible here because we have a precedent for handling this" or "I'll compromise because it's part of our organizational culture to work together to resolve these kind of issues."

5. **Your boss disapproves.** A great reason to stand firm is to prove to your higher-ups that you're determined to make waves and manage more boldly than your predecessors. While that's a worthy goal, make sure you'll truly impress your boss with your show of spine. If you report to a conciliator, however, then watch out! Your refusal to back down can work against you.

6. **Great results hang in the balance.** As a new manager, you cannot sacrifice bottom-line results in the name of winning a juvenile game of

"chicken." Backing down can work to your advantage if it enables you and your team to resume your work and achieve an important objective. The benefits of managing your staff to produce a resounding success—whether in terms of cost savings, productivity gains, or other high-visibility triumphs—easily outweigh the cost of retreating when you'd prefer to hold your ground.

These six scenarios do not represent an exhaustive list of all the times when it's smart to back down. As situations arise, you must examine your intent. Do you want to prove a point at all costs, even if it means alienating your employees or even bosses? Or do you want to display toughness by knowing when to fold your cards so that you win larger prizes in the future?

Myth 6: You're the Best Teacher

In exposing this myth, you need to accept one undeniable fact: you don't know everything.

Just because you're given a staff to manage doesn't make you their one and only teacher. You're not supposed to spoon-feed them knowledge so that they know everything that you know. As much as you may want to sit down with each employee and go over certain processes and procedures, you can't clone your know-how and pass it around like sticks of gum.

You're one of many sources of insight for your employees. That should give you a sense of relief. For starters, they'll learn from each other by osmosis. They'll absorb tips and techniques to work smarter simply through teaming up. They may also extract pointers from other executives, team leaders, and outside consultants.

This doesn't mean you should teach them the basic skills and then back off and let the rest take care of itself. You still need to create a learning environment and encourage employees to share ideas and teach each other. A useful way to plant the seeds of knowledge is to designate certain individuals to train others in a specific area. Examples: you send Jim to a database management course so that he in turn can help his coworkers understand this process, and you help Mary understand risk management so that she in turn can spread the word on worker safety and accident prevention. By turning key employees into experts, you can create a teaching corps so that your team essentially educates itself.

While you're not the best (or only) teacher for your employees, you can take steps to increase the amount of learning that takes place. Begin by encouraging your team to ask penetrating ques-

TAP IN-HOUSE KNOWLEDGE SMART

MANAGING

Savvy managers harness their employees' know-how by turning them into internal experts. Intranets make it easy: use your employer's in-house web network to launch a collaborative platform for workers to connect with peers to share best practices and answer each other's questions. In time, as your team builds a repository of practical information, workers will go online to seek insights from each other rather than look to you.

tions. At staff meetings, don't feel obliged to answer every one of their inquiries. Throw open the discussion and let participants bounce ideas off each other. Ideally, you want them to engage in their own search for answers in which they exchange information and observations.

Don't worry if such discussions veer off on tangents. The best teachers don't necessarily teach in the conventional sense; they sit back and guide others to dig for answers.

Another way to spread knowledge is to invite guest speakers to address your employees. These experts can come from other departments within your company or from the outside. Let them relate their experiences and findings on a topic that enlightens your workers. Choose subjects that your team has asked you about in the past; this shows that

LUNCH 'N' LEARN

FOR EXAMPLE

To foster a more lively learning environment, a new manager launched "lunch 'n' learn" sessions in his company's cafeteria. On the last Thursday of every month, employees were invited to bring their meal and listen to experts discuss a job-related skill. During the first six sessions, speakers covered topics ranging from public speaking tips to time management. The manager recruited local consultants to speak, offering them a free lunch and a chance to "rehearse" in front of company officials who might hire them in the future. Thus, the cost of the manager's program was minimal. And as word spread of these stimulating sessions, turnout soared.

you're responsive to the needs and willing to indulge their curiosity. If you embrace the myth that you're the best teacher for your employees, then you may fall into the trap of spouting platitudes and pretending to know more than you really do. What's worse, your team may tire of your pontificating and question your credibility. When workers start to doubt the accuracy of your remarks or dread your lectures, then you know you're overdoing it.

Remember: your job as manager isn't to teach employees everything they need to know. By letting them find their own way, you wind up with a more motivated, intelligent team.

New Manager's Checklist for Chapter 2

☑ Limit the decisions you make so that you delegate more responsibility to your staff.

☑ While it's unwise to blindly believe everything your employees tell you, give them chances to earn your trust.

☑ Radiate enthusiasm and express genuine feelings when appropriate. Don't bury your personality because you think managers cannot show emotion.

☑ Stand by your staff when the situation calls for it, but don't instinctively defend them from any and all criticism.

☑ Assess whether it's in your interest to back down rather than stubbornly cling to an untenable position.

☑ Give employees ample opportunities to learn from others rather than viewing you as their sole teacher.

Building Momentum in a New Job

Congratulations! You've been promoted. It's your first day as a new manager. You're wearing your best outfit, your hair is freshly cut, and you're ready to lead your staff to greatness.

You want to start on the right foot. Other managers have warned you that first impressions matter, so you want to make every effort to establish the right relationship with your employees from Day One. You also know that if you can gain credibility quickly, you'll find it easier to give instructions that others will follow.

It makes you nervous to think about it, but it's true: you're now under a microscope. Your employees—as well as your boss—will be scrutinizing your words and actions. As the cops tell suspects, anything you say can be used against you.

Consistency Counts

The best way to build momentum as a new manager is to make it clear to everyone what you stand for. Then follow through. Employees cannot help but respect a boss who begins by communicating a few core principles—and then exemplifies those principles in the weeks and months ahead.

That's why a management credo helps. As we discussed in Chapter 1, by preparing a summary that serves as your blueprint for how you intend to manage, you're less likely to fumble for direction as you get to know your employees. With a written credo as your reference, you can always remind yourself of the big picture: what you're trying to accomplish and how you intend to get the job done.

By showing from the outset that you're guided by unshakable, unassailable underlying beliefs, you eliminate much of the ambiguity and confusion that employees often resent in new managers. Workers often complain to me of supervisors who suddenly start acting like politicians as soon as they're put in charge of a staff.

You'll squander any traces of initial goodwill by trying to feed everyone what they want to hear or spouting platitudes about the kind of unit you want to run. Employees see through such meaningless drivel. They want straight answers. You make matters worse by pretending to know more than you do—or trying to overcompensate by appearing so confident that you border on arrogant and infallible.

In the opening weeks of your new job, it's important not to send contradictory signals or give different answers to the same question. That's a common rookie mistake. You'll stumble out of the gate if your employees approach you in an exasperated tone and say, "You said something else yesterday" or "I'm not sure if you've approved or denied my request." To avoid this, follow these three rules:

> **CAUTION**
>
> **WIMPING OUT**
>
> Most employees respond well to straight-talking managers. If you repeatedly respond to their concerns with mushy or evasive answers, such as "Let's revisit that later," "We'll see," or "I'll try my hardest," you'll bob and weave your way into oblivion. It's fine to say "I don't know," as long as you ask some fact-gathering questions and show interest in formulating a serious answer. That's the kind of consistency they'll appreciate.

1. **Don't improvise when you can repeat yourself.** Give simple answers to employees' questions, without inserting lots of asides. Provide the identical response as many times as necessary, even if two workers rephrase a similar question when they ask you. Don't feel obliged to editorialize or give new shadings to statements you've already made to others on the same topic.

2. **Don't oversell or overpromise.** Learn to consistently underpromise and overdeliver. That's better than hyping your latest proposal, only

to change your mind in a flash. Whenever you speculate about the future with your employees, err on the conservative side. Make modest commitments you're sure you can keep; then, if you wind up exceeding others' expectations, you'll be a hero.

3. **Don't fake it.** Never speak authoritatively on a subject you know nothing about. That sounds obvious, but many new managers dread having to admit what they don't know in the early weeks on the job. But there's no better way to build credibility than to acknowledge your limits and show a willingness to learn along with your employees.

A final point about consistency: don't play favorites. If you take over a management job where you're tempted to treat your longtime friends differently from everyone else, you're doomed to fail. Treat every individual the same. Drill home the same messages, give the same answers, and express the same goals regardless of which employee you're addressing.

Love at First Sight?

"I'll make one promise," said Sam as he introduced himself to his staff on his first day. "I'm always going to treat each of you the way I want to be treated. Let me tell you why. It's not that I'm a warm-and-fuzzy guy. No, the real reason is that one day, you may be my boss, and payback's a bitch."

The room erupted in laughter. Sam had his employees in the palm of his hand.

By making a favorable first impression with your employees, you make everything that follows much easier. You give yourself a wider margin for error later, because you persuade your people that you're a decent, fair-minded manager. Ideally, you want to leave your first meeting with your team by having them nod and say to one another, "Now *that's* a manager I can work for."

In the above remark, Sam pulls it off brilliantly. By stating one of his core principles in a humorous way, he achieves three goals:

1. He shows he doesn't take himself too seriously.
2. He implicitly compliments his employees by implying that they're talented enough to be his boss one day.
3. He makes a solemn promise without wasting words, thus magnifying the importance of his commitment.

Like Sam, you want to win over your staff from the beginning. With careful planning, you can make all the right moves.

Staging the First Meeting

If you want to get off to a running start with your employees, here are three words of advice: don't wing it. Plan every detail so that you create a supportive, nonthreatening atmosphere.

Even if you've met some of your staff individually, it's the first team meeting that sets the tone and serves as your true initiation. By making everyone feel comfortable, you build instant momentum and instill confidence in your leadership. Such meetings should occur on your first day, not a week or two into your job.

Prepare by making a list of questions that your employees may ask you. Include issues that individuals have already raised with you one-on-one. Plan responses to each question, noting key points you want to express. Test yourself by rehearsing your answers—ideally by recording them—and running them through a battery of tests:

- Did I say what I wanted to say?
- Did I use words and phrases that my employees will understand?
- Did I communicate clearly and concisely?

If you answered yes to all three questions, you're ready to proceed with confidence.

If possible, reserve a cozy conference room where everyone must sit near one another. That fosters a more close-knit feeling. If people are too scattered or retreat into their own space, you'll find it harder to rally them as a group. Plus, making eye contact is easier if people sit closer to you.

If you're nervous, don't fight it. Trying to hide your opening-day jitters won't work. Instead, accept your fears as a

CIRCLE IN THE SQUARE

Arrange the seats in a circle so that no one appears more senior than anyone else, including you. A classroom-style setting can create an invisible barrier between you and your staff, because the rows of seats may make employees feel like students (and they'll perceive you as the teacher/taskmaster). Same goes with a U-shaped conference setup with you at the head of the table.

healthy sign that you want to do well. Tell yourself, "The fact that I'm anxious tells me that I care about this job." The less you dwell on your nerves, the more you can occupy yourself with other, more pressing concerns—like connecting with your staff.

For example, it's common for new managers to get caught up in relatively minor worries on their first day, such as how they look or whether they remember everyone's name. Rid yourself of such petty concerns by taking some practical preventive steps. Choose the appropriate outfit a week in advance and make sure it's freshly cleaned and ironed. And ask your human resources manager for a list of your employees' names ahead of time—along with a photo and some brief biographical information—so that you can get a head start on getting to know them.

Don't call attention to your anxiety on your first day. If you flub the first few lines of your introductory speech, move on; avoid apologizing and starting from the beginning. If you make a faux pas, such as not hearing someone's name and calling him or her the wrong name, laugh easily and recover in a flash.

Remember: your employees will be nervous, too. They want to curry favor with you. They may sense you're a bit nervous, but they won't mind as long as you don't make a big deal about it. What will bother them is if they perceive that you're going out of your way to be mean or tough or somehow fake. The more authentic you appear, the better.

During this first meeting with your staff, resist the urge to volunteer too much information about yourself. Your short introduction should consist of no more than the basics: your relevant experience and your goals and expectations for your team. Rehearse this mini-speech in the days before your first day; if it's longer than three minutes, cut it.

HELLO, MY NAME IS ... SMART MANAGING

Begin the meeting by introducing yourself briefly. Then ask employees to introduce themselves by isolating a skill that they bring to their job. Tell them not to mention their present or past job titles, which can interfere with unity and imply power and seniority. As you go around the room, don't interrupt the speakers. But ask clarifying questions as needed, such as "How did you develop that skill?" Encourage other employees to do the same.

If your employer has already sent a "welcome aboard" memo to employees along with your bio, summarize a few of your career highlights, but don't repeat every line of your résumé. Assume that curious staffers have not only read the memo but also investigated you online. Conduct a web search on your name so that you see what they see about your background.

When you invite your employees to speak, don't keep tugging the conversation back to *you*. Some new managers arrive on their first day full of doubt and insecurity, and they relieve their angst by trying to play "topper" and bragging about their accomplishments every few minutes. That's a surefire way to pummel your employees into submission, rather than build momentum and excite your team about your leadership.

I, Me, Mine

CAUTION

You'll know that you're hogging the spotlight if you spend your first meeting talking about your experiences and spouting your opinions. Keep the personal reflections to a minimum, unless you're asked point-blank by an employee to share your views on a particular topic (and that's rare). Strive to limit your speaking to 10 percent of the meeting, thus allowing your employees to take center stage and bounce off each other's remarks.

Score a Quick Win

In the course of your first meeting with employees and subsequent one-on-one discussions, you should begin to identify the problems they care about most. This information tells you where to focus your efforts to produce early results.

There's no better way to establish momentum as a new manager than to show that you're responsive to your team's concerns. If they complain about the company's rigid bureaucracy, find a way to loosen up. If they confess that they're exhausted from overwork—and you conclude they're putting in far too many hours—relieve their burden by streamlining procedures, hiring more people, or temporarily tackling some of the overflow work yourself. Explore the benefits of enacting a Practical Process Improvement (PPI) program—a series of steps for work teams to continuously enhance operations, reduce waste, and maximize efficiency. If they need certain equipment to perform their jobs better, make every effort to acquire these tools quickly.

Here are some other ways you to endear yourself to employees and thus prolong your honeymoon period:

- **Remove long-standing irritants.** The longer something has plagued your employees, the more heroic you'll appear if you address it. As a new manager, you cannot be blamed for anything that predated your arrival. So in many cases you have nothing to lose by trying to play fixer when they propose reasonable solutions. Example: If customer service reps tell you they've repeatedly asked for an automated web-based system for tracking and updating client accounts, make it happen. If your bosses sit on your request, implement it on your own. Employees love having can-do mavericks for managers.

- **Simplify their lives.** Find a way to make your employees' jobs easier. Example: eliminate a needless procedure, give them more flexibility over their hours, stop e-mailing them on evenings and weekends.

- **Assign team leaders to recommend solutions.** Convening a team every time your employees mention a problem can get you into trouble, especially if you're not ready to act on their suggestions. But in your first weeks on the job, you can show you treat this approach seriously. Avoid acting like a politician who's scared of making a tough decision by distributing a precise timetable to each team leader (who's chosen by teammates, not by you). Present dates when you want to see a list of proposed solutions *and* commit to a date when you promise to respond. Then follow through.

In your eagerness to please your new staff, beware of giving too much away. Employees who think you're a pushover may take advantage of your kindness by upping

BE BOLD ON DAY ONE

FOR EXAMPLE

On the day that Paul Polman became chief executive of Unilever in 2009, he made an instant splash. He announced that the global consumer products company would no longer provide earnings guidance and quarterly profit reports, breaking a long-standing custom. Reflecting on his bold move four years later, Polman told *Fortune* magazine, "I figured that the day they hired me, they can't fire me, so that was probably the best moment to do that."

the ante. The more you do for them, the more they might ask. Then you're stuck in a never-ending spiral of granting concessions, approving expenditures, and compromising your objectives to accommodate employees' whims.

The whole point of scoring quick wins is to generate momentum and assert your leadership. You must still choose your battles and guard against overindulging your employees. If you give them too much too soon, you will set yourself up to fail over the long run.

Unclog "Input Channels"

After their first month, I like to ask new managers to describe in one word their experience so far. The number one answer: alone.

They often tell me that as much as they think they're off to a good start, they have no idea how they're doing. They cannot confide in a staff member, because they fear they won't get a straight answer. And their hands-off boss may not pay much attention or offer much encouragement in the early weeks. That leaves these fledgling managers to shrug and assume they're doing okay, without gathering input from others.

To avoid falling into a black hole of uncertainty, you need to flood yourself with feedback from all sides. That probably won't happen on its own. When you're new on the job and you stumble out of the gate, you may not even realize that something's amiss unless someone tells you. In blissful ignorance, you may figure that everything's copacetic. Then you're stunned to learn that your staff is lining up against you and your boss already doubts your judgment.

To prevent this, you need input channels. By collecting helpful feedback on how you're doing, you can make adjustments before it's too late.

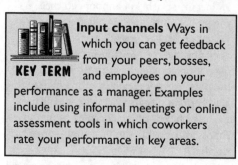

Input channels Ways in which you can get feedback from your peers, bosses, **KEY TERM** and employees on your performance as a manager. Examples include using informal meetings or online assessment tools in which coworkers rate your performance in key areas.

To establish input channels, you must make it easy for others throughout your organization to give their input. Most bosses and subordinates will not give you a running commentary on your performance. Even if you ask for feedback, they may not necessarily provide the kind of revealing, honest answers you want.

Here are three ways to probe for information on how you're doing:

1. **Formalize the process.** Work with your human resources team on developing 360-degree feedback mechanisms. These systems enable colleagues at all levels to give input, sometimes anonymously, on an individual's performance. About 85 percent of Fortune 500 companies use 360-degree feedback, according to Zenger Folkman, a leadership development firm. Typically, respondents will share their perceptions of the subject's ability to motivate, willingness to listen, and effectiveness in managing time and prioritizing key tasks. An advantage of gathering feedback from multiple sources is you can spot trends and address them sooner rather than later. If you learn that your short attention span and tendency to interrupt annoy some members of your team, you can develop more focus and listen more patiently.

2. **Seek casual advice.** In the first few months as a manager, show plenty of interest in your employees' ideas and opinions. The more you get them to share their thoughts, the more likely they'll open up to you about your performance. Say, "You've given me a lot to think about, but one area we haven't discussed is your impression so far of my management style. Can you give me some input?"

3. **Trace changes in behavior.** As you get to know your employees, watch how they relate to you. Note their body language. Do they smile and seem comfortable chatting with you? Do they volunteer comments when they run into you in the hall? Do they station themselves near you in a meeting or try to keep a low profile? Armed with these observations, monitor changes in the first month or two on the job. If you notice someone no longer seems as eager to stop and chat in the lunchroom, for instance, you may want to get input as to why.

To unclog input channels, prepare to listen without lashing out. Accept that you may hear things that surprise and upset you. But rather than react negatively, maintain your equanimity. This way, you condition your employees to "tell it like it is" without fear of recrimination or backlash.

TRICKS OF THE TRADE

ASK THE RIGHT QUESTION

Wording counts when you seek feedback. Never ask an employee, "Can you give me any feedback?" It's smarter to say "I'd like to hear all your feedback." Reason: the word *any* needlessly narrows the scope of the question. The employee may only give you one minor piece of advice to satisfy your inquiry. But by wording your question more broadly, you indicate that you expect a longer, more thorough response.

I'm always reminding new managers that the input they get from employees is priceless, whether they like to hear it or not. By absorbing it in a graceful manner, they guard against self-delusion. They'll never let their performance sink too deep as long as they're aware of what needs to improve.

The worst response is defensiveness. Resist the urge to justify your behavior. You don't want others to think "Why bother giving honest feedback to someone who's not going to take it to heart?"

Instead, dig to learn as much as you can from others. In an earnest tone, seek examples. Ask questions such as "Are there certain situations when I do this more or less often?" or "How long have you noticed me doing this?"

The more input channels you establish, the more prudent risks you'll take. If you know how your employees perceive you, that can give you the confidence to have them experiment with new ways to work. You'll also lead more dynamically if you're aware of what your team likes and doesn't like about how you communicate and motivate them.

GIVE ME MORE

FOR EXAMPLE

Dave's employees freely told him how they felt about his management approach. From the day he started as manager, he vowed to treat every piece of input as a gold nugget. When he asked for feedback, he took unpleasant news with good cheer by thinking, "I'm so lucky to learn this now, not later." When employees mentioned issues that Dave deemed unfair or beyond his control, he thought, "It's not their job to tell me how to correct my performance, just to share their honest thoughts with me." After his employees gave input, Dave automatically would reply, "Thank you. Please, go on." And they would say even more thanks to his gentle prodding.

If you fail to get feedback, then you can start off on the wrong foot and tumble downhill from there. You want to generate that head of steam, but nothing seems to work. You may begin to sense that you're struggling, so you fall into the rookie manager trap of resting on your laurels. You retreat into what you know best: your technical strengths or professional expertise. But now that you're a manager, those skills no longer will save you. You need to expand your repertoire by finding new people management tools, not just rely on what's worked when you were on your own.

Are You Ready for Anything?

Nothing kills momentum like a flaring crisis. It can arise out of nowhere and deplete everyone's energy for days at a time.

While you cannot possibly put out every fire before it ignites, you can take steps to reduce the risk. This requires a high level of readiness. By anticipating what can go wrong and devising a strategy to guard against it, you impose at least some order on an otherwise disorderly universe of work-related mishaps.

When you first get promoted into management, schedule meetings with other managers who've had the job you're about to take. If you're ascending into a newly designed job with no predecessors, interview individuals who hold similar positions either inside or outside your organization.

Use these meetings to get acquainted with the types of challenges you can expect to confront in the early going. Ask questions such as:

- In your first six months in that job, what was your biggest surprise?
- What was the worst crisis you ever faced in the job? What was the worst crisis in the first six months?
- If you wish you could have

OUTSIDER HELP

A great way to anticipate crises that can derail your early progress is to interview key vendors, suppliers, and consultants who are familiar with the job you're starting. Ask them what kinds of pitfalls may be ahead for you. Encourage them to share their impressions of your predecessor and discuss the highs and lows of their dealings with your team. Solicit their ideas on how your business unit can boost efficiency, unclog communication channels, or improve performance.

known one thing about the job before you took it, what would that be?

■ What steps did you take early on that helped minimize problems down the line? What steps do you wish you had taken?

As you gather answers, you can begin to spot potential trouble spots. A seasoned manager may warn you not to trust the weekly activity reports or to devote at least a few hours a week keeping key colleagues "in the loop." If managers in another department tend to feel ignored or taken for granted, for example, they may not cooperate as much and make your life harder once you take over. Knowing this now can give you a heads-up on how to manage more effectively from Day One.

Aside from picking the brains of your employees, peers, and key outsiders, don't forget your boss. Realize, however, that the executive whom you report to won't necessarily have hands-on awareness of the kind of fires that can flare in your new job. At large organizations, senior executives are often removed from the daily operational realities of management positions (although they might not want to admit that!).

In any case, inform your boss that you want to hit the ground running as a new manager, free of any avoidable crises in the early months. Solicit advice and try to uncover problems that can erupt soon after you start.

As an added precaution, submit a list of challenges that you expect to face in your new job. Review this list with your boss. Examples might include "train employees to use new risk analysis system" or "negotiate new lease contracts." As you discuss each item, work with your boss to identify what can go wrong and what preventive steps you can take. Your boss won't necessarily give you all the answers, but may at least guide you to approach potential crises in a calm, sensible manner and think of ways to reduce your risk.

Finally, train your employees to anticipate problems and address them in advance. Explain to them that some fires cannot be prevented, and you will need to save all of your team's energy and resourcefulness to put out the flames. Then add that for those problems that you and your staff *can* control, it's vital to get ready now and reduce the odds of needless hassles later.

To increase everyone's preparedness, ask your employees what kind of crises they found to be the most disruptive before you arrived. Most workers love to talk about what can go wrong, and they may give you ample suggestions on how to plan for worst-case scenarios.

If they don't have many tales of woe and hardship from the past, try asking them, "What crisis do you fear the most?" This may unleash a few doom-and-gloom comments, but that's what you want. Ideally, you should come away with a much better understanding of the kind of snafus that can destroy the progress that you and your staff intend to make in the months ahead.

New Manager's Checklist for Chapter 3

☑ Send clear, consistent signals in your early months as manager. Express your core principles and key goals and stick to them.

☑ If you don't know something, admit it. Employees will appreciate your honesty, and you'll earn credibility.

☑ Make a strong first impression by holding a staff meeting on your first day as manager. Leave plenty of time for employees to introduce themselves and discuss their strengths.

☑ Chalk up a quick win that endears you to your employees. Examples include removing a much-hated bureaucratic process or arranging for workers to have better tools or equipment.

☑ Make it easy for your employees to give you feedback. Give them many ways to communicate their input to you and respond to it gracefully.

☑ Put out fires before they begin by anticipating what can go wrong and devising appropriate strategies.

Managing to Listen

N ow that you're a manager, you can interrupt employees freely. If you don't like what you hear—or you think they're wrong—you can jump in and say so.

Before you bask in your newfound power, however, weigh the consequences of rushing to judge what others say. Your refusal to listen can come back to bite you.

As president of The Coca-Cola Co., Donald Keough was visiting the beverage giant's German operations soon after the Berlin Wall fell in 1989. In a meeting with Coke's top German executives, Keough heard them propose a $500 million investment in the newly democratized East Germany. Keough dismissed the idea outright.

After the meeting, Keough learned that the head of German operations wanted to resign. The executive felt that Keough didn't listen to his proposal and rejected it without even letting him finish his presentation.

To his credit, Keough convened another meeting and listened without interruption. This time, he was sold. At the World Economic Forum in Davos, Switzerland, just one month later, he announced that Coca-Cola would invest $1 billion in Eastern Europe, including East Germany.

As Keough writes in his 2008 book, *The 10 Commandments for Business Failure*, that decision not only proved profitable for Coca-Cola but opened the former Soviet bloc countries to receive further Western investment.

Keough's story reminds us of the crucial need to listen, especially to subordinates' ideas and concerns. Many first-time managers think that it's up to them to do most of the talking. They've already paid their dues by biting their lip and pretending not to mind when a boss interrupted them or monopolized their time by telling long, boastful stories. Now it's their turn to dominate—to control conversations by blabbing at will.

Many people equate listening with subservience and speaking with authority. That can lead managers to talk louder and more forcefully than everyone else in the room. They can grow attached to the sound of their own voice, convinced that they've reached the promised land where they can repeat themselves at will, crack their favorite jokes, and interrupt underlings with impunity.

In fact, your listening skills count even more now that you're in charge. Your ability to observe others and extract valuable information from them will help you persuade them. Your willingness to stay attentive even when you're tired or distracted will help you build trust. And your commitment to interpret and assess what you hear rather than capture it at face value will save you from costly misunderstandings.

By establishing a baseline of how you listen, you can identify barriers to clear communication. This awareness enables you to take steps to overcome your vulnerabilities so that you become a stronger, more resilient listener.

Circle all statements that describe how you communicate:

- I'm more of a talker than a listener.
- I find it harder to listen when I become highly emotional.
- I often find myself faking it: pretending to listen while I'm really thinking about other things.
- I usually try to listen while I think of what I want to say next.
- I'm a selective listener: I pay more attention to speakers whom I respect.
- My mind wanders almost immediately when I must listen to a babbler.
- I often interrupt people who repeat themselves.
- I'm a multitasker: I can listen while texting or glancing at my smartphone.

Each of the statements that you circled indicates a potential trouble spot. But don't worry that you're doing anything bad or wrong. Many of the new managers I train tend to fret if they circle three or four of the above items. They assume that they're hopelessly weak listeners who need remedial help. Rest assured it's common for people to recognize some if not all of these statements. The key is to build on this awareness-raising exercise and find strategies to sharpen your listening skills.

Let's get started.

Tapping the Power of Silence

Many managers admit that they're poor listeners. They confess to me that if they could just keep their mouth shut, they would build better rapport with their employees, stop themselves from making mistaken assumptions, and avoid jumping to conclusions.

They tell me how badly they listen—over and over again! I'm often subject to rambling monologues in which managers berate themselves for sloppy listening. After making their point abundantly clear, they pause to take a breath and ask me, "Does this make any sense?"

"Oh, yeah," I nod. "I see the problem."

In short, they don't know when to "say when." They lapse into motor-mouth mode, stringing their words together to create an oral traffic jam with no apparent end.

It's not enough to acknowledge that you could improve how you listen. The first step on the road to improvement is simple: keep quiet.

Using silence well doesn't automatically make you a better listener. After all, you can daydream while pretending to pay attention to your employees' comments. But if you're trying to guide staffers to think

APPLY THE BRAKES
The next time you're about to interrupt a speaker, don't. Force yourself to clam up. To ensure you don't cut someone off, silently count to three before you respond. That way, you insert a cushion of silence into the conversation. At that point, don't be surprised if the speaker chimes in again. Managers often learn the most revealing facts from their employees only *after* they stay silent an extra few moments. An employee who's hiding something may spill the beans if you don't rush to interrupt.

for themselves—rather than look to you for instant answers—then your silence will show that you're willing to wait and hear what they have to say. By sitting still without constantly hogging the conversation, you send a message that you're not going to do the mental legwork for them.

This works particularly well when you're helping an employee make a tough decision. Rookie managers can construct an airtight argument and list dozens of superb reasons why they think a worker should act a certain way. But that won't necessarily sway an ambivalent person. You may need to let the individual talk it out to grow truly convinced of the proper course of action.

The worst listeners use words as weapons. They may assume that if they can drown employees in facts, opinions, or examples, they will overcome their team's objections and gain compliance. The truth is the reverse: it's by pouring on the silence that you enable others to decide that you're right.

FOR EXAMPLE

It's Sure Quiet in Here

Adam Jaworski, a professor of language and communication at the University of Hong Kong, has researched the role of silence in conversation. He finds that silence can work for or against you, depending on your relationship with others. Longtime colleagues or friends can grow accustomed to silence with each other without feeling uncomfortable. It can reinforce feelings of trust, security, and intimacy. But if you're a new manager just getting to know your team, inserting too many pauses might make others think you're hiding something.

When you're managing employees, remember that it's up to them to decide what to do. If you order them around indefinitely, you'll turn them into mindless drones. That means you need to use patience and eye contact, rather than firing off a fusillade of commands. Plus, you'll exert more influence by allowing them to speak freely. Don't feel obliged to reply to everything they say. Just let them think out loud and show silent, intent interest.

What's to Learn?

Mike Nichols, the director of movies ranging from *The Graduate* to *Charlie Wilson's War*, recently said, "People, by and large, would rather be talking than listening." As proof, he mentioned in a 2012 *Vanity Fair* interview that his wife, Diane Sawyer, travels the globe covering news events. He marveled that even if she's just returned from Afghanistan or Iraq to her home in New York, "no one ever asks her about what she saw."

What Nichols may not realize is that asking questions—and showing curiosity in others—requires mental discipline. If you're not listening as raptly as you'd like, the problem boils down to the fact that you're giving yourself permission to tune out. The real test is whether you can bear down and concentrate on what others tell you, even if it takes Herculean effort.

To train yourself to be more attentive, you need to step back and remind yourself *why* you bother to listen in the first place. The answer: you want to learn something.

Consider what happens when a boss walks into your office and praises you for excellent work. You're all ears. You listen because you like the message and you want to hear more. You're not about to let your mind wander or interrupt at your first opportunity.

But when an employee raises an issue that's not particularly interesting or important to you, the last thing you want to do is drop whatever else you're thinking about so that you can give the speaker your undivided attention. You assume you have more to gain by not listening all that carefully, so you only make a halfhearted stab at going through the motions.

Here's a better way: commit to learning at least one fact or opinion from every employee you speak with today. Begin every conversation with a determination to come away with fresh ideas or insights that you collect from others.

The more you listen to learn, the easier it'll become. Curiosity begets more curios-

> **TEACH ME, TEACH ME**   SMART
>
> In order to listen better and learn from others, you must thirst for knowledge. To arouse your curiosity the   **MANAGING** next time you're feeling bored or restless, think to yourself, "Teach me, teach me" while you're listening to your employees. By repeating this phrase silently, you'll listen with more openness and absorb more information. Make this your mantra, and you'll find yourself speaking less and listening more.

ity, and you'll experience a snowball effect as you start to capture a speaker's hopes, beliefs, and concerns with precision and accuracy. Once you begin to collect facts and opinions, you'll want to confirm them. That will lead you to ask follow-up questions and listen even more carefully to the answers.

The Three Steps of Listening

Hearing and listening are entirely different.

Hearing refers to a physical act: your ears receive sound waves. As one of your senses like seeing and touching, it doesn't require any real effort. That's why it's so easy to take for granted.

Listening, by contrast, tests your mental focus. You need to go beyond sensing incoming sounds so that you process what you hear. This unfolds in three steps: interpreting, assessing and responding.

Interpreting

Once you hear something, you need to make sure you understand the message that the words convey. This involves a kind of quick mental translation in which you take what you hear and rephrase it in your own words.

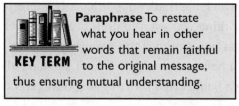

Paraphrase To restate what you hear in other words that remain faithful to the original message, thus ensuring mutual understanding.

KEY TERM

A newly installed manager will often bring different vocabulary, experiences, and biases to a conversation with an employee. This can lead to crossed signals and mismatched messages. For example, if an entry-level worker tries to warn you of a problem by saying, "I'm not so sure about that" to your suggestion, you can interpret that to mean:

■ I don't want to comply with your suggestion.
■ I doubt you're right.
■ I have more information to share with you if you pry it out of me.
■ I don't know as much about this as you do, so I defer to you.

You must clarify what the employee means before you respond. Each possible interpretation has its own subtle shadings. Unless you follow up in a pleasant, nonthreatening tone, you may judge the employee's remark unfairly and draw the wrong conclusion.

A foolproof way to check your interpretation of what someone says is to repeat what you heard verbatim, but as a question. In the above example, you would respond, "You're not so sure about that?"

Speak in a neutral, curious manner; don't adopt an accusatory or angry voice. You'll find that the employee reveals more, thus enabling you to listen accurately and interpret the message as it was intended.

If you try to listen when you're angry or preoccupied, you may find it hard to interpret what you hear properly. That's all the more reason to repeat what others tell you as a question. Your moods and even your physiological state can affect whether speakers' words mean the same thing to you as they do to them.

Assessing

After you interpret a message, you get to judge it.

Poor or impatient listeners often skip the interpretation stage. They rush to evaluate what they hear, stamping messages with mental labels such as "right," "wrong," "smart," or "stupid." They instantly decide whether a speaker's comments are "worth it." They dismiss anything that strikes them negatively.

New managers are particularly susceptible to this trap. They may read too much into what their employees tell them and decide how they will use (or not use) the information they gather before they confirm they heard it correctly.

The best way to assess what you hear is to remain open-minded. Rather than box yourself in by thinking, "This makes no sense" or "This information doesn't help me at all," judge messages more charitably.

BAD ASSESSING = BAD NEWS

Beware of evaluating messages based solely on whether you like or don't like what you hear. If you judge an employee's remarks harshly from the moment he opens his mouth, that will influence how you listen. Do not disregard information just because you're ticked off by the nature or topic of the message. Overcome that obstacle. Accurately assess what your employee wants you to know. Evaluate it based on a dispassionate analysis of the facts, not a gut reaction or snap judgment.

CAUTION

Consider all sides of an issue. While you should still apply critical reasoning skills and listen attentively to every word, remain flexible and keep digging for information. Assessing works best when you're willing to reverse your judgments and reconsider firmly held assumptions or beliefs.

Responding

The first two stages of listening occur inside your head. You mentally translate a speaker's comment to gain understanding. Then you judge its value. Now it's time to let the world know that you're listening.

Your employees won't know if you've received their messages unless you respond. This is an external act, a way of signaling your willingness to listen.

Your response can be oral or visual. The most common way to respond is to say something such as "I understand" or "Please go on." If you want to test the accuracy of your interpretation, you can restate what you hear as a question as we discussed above.

As a rule, it's smart not to respond by immediately presenting your point of view. Most employees want bosses who listen raptly and don't rush to interrupt. You'll earn their trust more quickly by responding with a follow-up question or a "prod statement" that invites them to talk some more.

> **KEY TERM**
>
> **Prod statement** A brief remark that prompts speakers to continue. You can elicit more information and gently prod them to elaborate with statements such as "This is interesting," "I see," or "Tell me more." Always follow a prod statement with silence. This gives the speaker permission to go on and shows that you're really intent on hearing more.

You can also respond to a speaker with nonverbal cues. The most obvious examples are vigorous nods, beaming smiles, or severe frowns. Shaking your head in disgust or disagreement can indicate your displeasure, but it can also drive away employees who would otherwise come to you with their ideas or concerns.

The best listening response is to maintain eye contact while showing interest in the speaker. Too much nodding and gesturing can actually distract an employee who's trying to tell you something.

"My manager starts nodding her head the moment I start talking," says a loan officer. "I start to talk faster, because I feel she's nodding because she wants me to get to my point quicker. It makes me uncomfortable."

When I met this person's boss, I thought that her frequent nodding was really a nervous tic. She would nod almost all the time, regardless of the speaker. She wasn't even aware of it. I put a small mirror near her desk in an unobtrusive position so that she could see for herself. After two days, she agreed she bobbed her head too much when she listened. Thanks to some relaxation exercises, she learned to keep still and respond more with eye contact than constant nodding.

We'll explore other aspects of listeners' body language in the pages that follow.

Fighting Off the Defensive Reflex

When you cook an elaborate meal, you may not like what you serve. All your hard work won't necessarily guarantee a splendid feast that you and your guests find delicious.

Same goes with listening. Even if you're rapt and attentive, you may not like what you hear. The message can rub you the wrong way, and your irritation can block out what follows.

The more you practice good listening skills, the sooner you'll learn to stay tuned to both positive and negative comments. You'll develop the discipline to assess the content of a speaker's remarks without instantly reacting.

New managers are particularly susceptible to the defensive reflex. When an employee complains or criticizes, it's a common trap for a novice supervisor to cut in with phrases such as "Hear me out a second" or "You've got it wrong."

Defensive reflex The reflexive urge to defend yourself against attack when you hear something **KEY TERM** that upsets you. Rather than pausing, letting the message sink in, and confirming understanding, you rush to contradict or justify your position. This defensive posture weakens your ability to listen.

There's a time and place for asserting your views or correcting a misperception. But first, you must demonstrate to your staffers that you've heard them. That takes patience. If they want to get something off their chest, then let them. Don't feel you must say a word. Your presence alone can show that you're willing to listen.

Before you defend yourself or mount a defense on behalf of others such as your organization's senior management, check to make sure you can make an impact. Here's a quick test to tell if you're on safe ground shifting into defensive mode:

1. You've let the speaker gab at will. You have not tried to rush, prod, or interrupt. You have not finished his sentences or shown visible impatience such as glancing at the clock.

2. You've asked at least one question to indicate your desire to learn more.

3. You've confirmed understanding by getting the other person to nod and acknowledge that you've accurately paraphrased the message.

In your first few months as a new manager, you'll undoubtedly experience one of the most frustrating aspects of human communication: not being understood. You'll struggle to make a point, plead with an employee, rephrase or repackage your suggestions, and, if you get really annoyed, lose your cool. And chances are you'll be defending yourself and your actions the entire time.

Here are five simple words to help you combat this problem: listen for understanding, not agreement.

> **SMART MANAGING**
>
> **"PAC" It In**
>
> When you want to avoid the defensive reflex, remember the acronym PAC. It stands for Patience-Ask-Confirm, and it corresponds to the three-prong test described above. As long as you've demonstrated patience, asked at least one question, and confirmed that you've understood the speaker accurately, then you're in a much better position to respond forcefully.

Strive to prove to your employees that you appreciate what they're saying and how they're feeling. Rather than go through the motions with fake smiles and listless gestures, align yourself with them and let them drive the pace of the conversation. Get them to say—or at least think— "Yes, you understand me."

DEFENDING WITHOUT WORDS

You can lapse into the defensive reflex without saying a thing. Examples of silent but deadly actions that can drive a wedge into your relationships with employees:

CAUTION

- You shake your head vigorously while they're speaking as if to say "No, no, no."
- You hold up your hand like a traffic cop, trying to get them to stop talking.
- You roll your eyes, grimace in disgust, or otherwise appear like you want to put a sock in the speaker's mouth.

The moment you start to defend, you erect a barrier. Your attempt to listen turns into a battle between your effort to understand someone else and your misguided need to prove you're right, smart, or blameless. That's a fight you'll never win. Even if you satisfy your need to state your case, you may wind up talking to a brick wall. Your employees will tune out and walk away convinced that you just don't listen.

How's Your Body Language?

You can be the best listener on earth, but if you start fiddling with your tablet computer's touchscreen just as your employee opens up to you, then you'll lose the connection. Use your eyes to show that you listen. Plant them on the speaker and nowhere else.

Think how you feel when you're trying to communicate with someone who appears distracted. You're trying to drill home an important point, and you begin to feel like you're interacting with a disinterested, detached shell of a person. You notice these trouble signs:

- **A wandering eye.** Rather than look at you most of the time, the listener's eyes dart about nervously. You may notice the person look away to see who's walking by or what text messages pop up on his or her smartphone.
- **A physical preoccupation.** Rather than listen calmly, others are constantly scratching their necks or arms, rubbing their eyes, running their hand through their hair—perhaps even primping in front of you.
- **Yawning.** If someone looks tired, you've got to prune the deadwood

and cut straight to the crux of your message. You can sense that the more you talk, the less good it does.

Remember how irritated you would feel when you want to make yourself heard and the other person doesn't seem present? That should motivate you to listen more intently and send the right signals that you're ready, willing, and able to soak it all in.

FOR EXAMPLE

TURNING AROUND A BASKET CASE

I advised a jittery executive how to improve his body language so that his employees didn't feel neglected when they spoke with him. After years of getting feedback that he was "easily distracted" and stuck with a "short attention span," he wanted to shape up. After observing his behavior, I isolated three ways for him to improve:

1. **Face the speaker.** He had a bad habit of turning slightly to his side when he was listening. As a result, employees assumed he was somehow objecting to their comments or was bored or standoffish.
2. **Look into eyeballs.** He thought he gave great eye contact. But when I chatted with him, he kept looking at my forehead. If was as if I had a pimple that fascinated him. I coached him to lower his gaze slightly so that it met others' eyes.
3. **Keep your hands free.** He always liked to play with his pen. When others spoke, he would absentmindedly flip it, click it, and sometimes roll it across his desk back and forth.

As you listen, lean slightly toward the speaker if you're more than a few feet away. This reinforces your desire to hear every word. This works especially well if you run into an employee on a noisy hallway or factory floor and you start chatting. Show that you actually *want* to listen.

New Manager's Checklist for Chapter 4

☑ Before you respond, count silently to three. This prevents you from interrupting, and it allows the speaker to elaborate or reveal more information.

☑ Train yourself to listen better by striving to learn at least one fact or opinion from every conversation.

☑ Interpret, assess, and respond to what you hear in a patient, systematic way. Don't jump right to the third step and respond prematurely.

☑ Apply the PAC method to avoid instantly defending yourself when you hear criticism: Patiently listen, ask at least one question, and confirm that you've heard the speaker accurately.

☑ Listen for understanding, not agreement. Make room for differences in opinion or outlook.

☑ Align yourself with a speaker and maintain friendly eye contact so that your body language signals that you want to listen.

Speaking Like a Leader

After two months as a manager, Barbara met with her friend Sally to get some feedback on her performance as a boss. Even though the two women started as aides in the same department, Sally now reported to Barbara.

"Barbara, you talk differently now than you did before you were a manager," Sally said. "You sound a bit stiff, and your natural warmth doesn't come across like it used to. It's like you take everything you say so seriously."

That in a nutshell is the biggest trap new managers face: they try to speak the way they think a boss "should speak." That may mean adopting a deeper voice, giving unsolicited opinions, or issuing commands to display their authority.

Yet the best way to radiate power is to express it naturally. There's no one "right" speaking style. You don't have to give stirring speeches or crack jokes on cue. The more genuine you come across, the more you can make yourself clear and generate buy-in from your staff.

A Voice That Roars

For the first few days as a new manager, people will judge you like you've never been judged before. Like students checking out a substitute teacher, your employees will watch your every move and draw quick conclusions about your poise and leadership.

You're probably thinking, "In that case, I'd better dress just right, learn everyone's name, and not say anything stupid."

Fair enough. Yet the one tool you may take for granted—your voice—can influence how your employees perceive you more than any other single factor. This is the glaring detail that almost always gets overlooked by managers who are trying to sharpen their communication skills.

CHANGING THE WEATHER

CAUTION

Before you get too preoccupied with what you deem as the defects of your voice, step back and consider the bigger picture: if you communicate with authenticity and enthusiasm, no one's going to care about your vocal quirks. A CEO once told me that managers can "change the weather" for their employees by speaking in a sunny, bright manner. But if you exhibit a dark, stormy mood and grumble rather than speak, you'll spread dark clouds of gloom around you.

A bad voice can misrepresent you. It can alienate your staff, undermine your credibility, and betray your true feelings. It can even cause you physical pain if you don't treat it properly.

This doesn't mean you need to consult with a speech coach on pitch, tone, volume, tempo, and breath control. While each of these elements helps you speak dynamically, your primary goal as a new manager is simply to make your voice work for you, not against you.

Your Own Worst Enemy?

Ruth and Scott were both appointed to manage different parts of the information technology department at a large bank. I was training them on skills they'd need as new managers, when we got around to discussing the need for clear, commanding communication.

"I'm already in trouble," Ruth said. "Next week, Scott and I are going to address our employees. Scott goes first, and he's got this deep, powerful voice. Then I'll get up there, and people will strain to hear me. I'll sound really weak."

I told Ruth the good news. Her voice could actually prove a tremendous asset—not a liability. Her clear enunciation and self-assured pacing would draw listeners in, not drive them away.

"You don't have to try to sound like Scott," I replied. "It's a fact that men and women sound different. The key is to make yourself understood and to use your voice to reinforce your message."

You're not necessarily the best judge of your voice. I've heard nervous managers confess that they feared their first day in a new job because they would sound too mousy, too mean, too scared, too dull, too strict, or too bossy. I've heard them insist they had a terrible accent, a natural whisper, a chronically hoarse throat, or an embarrassing lisp.

Yet from the hundreds of managers I've advised, only

> ### STAGE A REALITY CHECK
> **TOOLS**
> Create a four-column worksheet with the following headings: volume, tempo, inflection, clarity. Send a copy of the worksheet to three trusted friends or colleagues. Now rate your voice on a 1-to-10 scale in each of these categories with 10 the best. Ask your three associates to do the same, encouraging them to be completely honest. Leave room on the page for them to explain their ratings or include additional feedback on your voice. Review their "score sheets" and compare them to your own. Evaluate to what extent you perceive your voice the same as others do.

about 1 percent were right to worry about their voice. These few individuals *did* have a problem that needed fixing. Everyone else convinced themselves they sounded far worse than they actually did.

But don't get complacent. You may sound better than you give yourself credit for, but you can still improve. First, practice your inflection. Emphasize only those words that you want to highlight. Beware of ending declarative sentences with an upward inflection; this can lead your staffers to think you doubt what you say. When you ask a question, make sure to inflect downward on the last word; this indicates you're now going to keep quiet and await an answer.

Also pay attention to projection, especially when you're addressing a group. Always begin talking to the individual seated farthest from you. This ensures that you speak loudly enough for everyone else to hear.

Remember to pause frequently so that you don't string words together. Fast talkers often get into trouble by trying to pack too much in at once. If you're explaining something or repeating lots of information, don't assume that just because it's familiar to you it'll sound equally familiar to your employees.

Packaging Your Points

As the boss, what you say goes. But if you bark too many orders without trying to explain your thinking or educate your staff, then you risk turning into a tyrant.

When you speak to employees, your goal should be to express your points in a way that makes it easy for them to understand you. If you hop from topic to topic in a disorderly fashion, you can leave a trail of confusion and noncompliance in your wake.

To present your points in an easy-to-understand manner, think before you speak. By sifting through what you want to say and selecting only the most relevant, timely comments, you avoid overloading your employees with too many details. You also help ensure that you say what you need to say.

 It's Not Too Late
The French have an expression that refers to all the clever and observant things you think to say after you part company with someone: *esprit d'escalier.* There's nothing more frustrating than realizing you forgot to warn or advise an employee about a key issue, and then wishing you could replay the conversation and get it right. By mapping out what you want to say ahead of time, you can avoid the regret that comes with lamenting the points that went unsaid.

Many new managers assume they know how to make themselves clear. They take communication for granted. Rather than pause and plan what they want to say, they plunge right in and eventually get around to the main point—babbling the whole time. They wing it and force their employees to struggle to figure out what's been said.

There's a better way. It involves thinking in threes, or breaking down your remarks into three distinct parts. You'll find that your staff can readily grasp ideas that come grouped in three. You might say, "There are three steps to this process," "I have three reasons for asking you to do this," or "Let's evaluate this idea on three different levels." By using such phrases, your listeners will know what's coming: You're about to deliver a trio of points to support your premise.

Clustering your remarks in threes works especially well when you want to persuade your employees to buy into your ideas. They'll find it harder to argue or rebut your points if you deliver three appropriate forms of support. Providing only one or two facts or assertions to back up your position may not prove too convincing, but when you add a third strand of evidence you can shut down potential resistance.

David Blair, former chief executive of Catalyst Health Solutions, told me that he wanted his 1,800 employees to demonstrate accountability, communication, and trust. He repeatedly reminded them that he prized these three traits. In 2009, he went a step farther: he created a company-wide ACT as a Team program, using an acronym (ACT—Accountability, Communication, Trust)) to reinforce the three qualities he sought to instill in his workforce. He emblazoned the slogan on coffee mugs and posters throughout the office. He even launched Caught in the ACT awards to recognize employees who held themselves accountable, communicated well, and showed trust in others when it counted.

Blair's ability to encapsulate his message in threes paid off. After many years of fast growth and industry-leading client retention rates, Catalyst Health Solutions merged with another firm in 2012 to become Catamaran Corp., a leading pharmacy benefit management company.

In another example of thinking in threes, Rhode Island Governor Lincoln Chafee announced a plan in 2012 to grow the state's economy by focusing on "the three Ts" of technology, talent, and tolerance. To attract young, creative people to live in the Ocean State, Chafee sought to support high-tech enterprises and employees with relevant job skills. He also championed same-sex marriage to honor what he called the state's "legacy of tolerance." By clustering the three Ts, he delivered a memorable message that resonated with voters.

You can speak with more authority by harnessing the

PLEAD AN AIRTIGHT CASE

FOR EXAMPLE

When Ron, a new manager, tried to persuade his 10 employees to fill out activity reports, they balked and gave excuses. Then he said, "There are three reasons why I'd like you to complete these reports. One, you'll find they help you get more done in less time, thus allowing you to get home at a reasonable hour. Two, you'll learn what obstacles keep you from spending more time on your favorite projects. And three, you'll qualify for incentive raises, because I intend to use these reports as one way to evaluate you."

power of three. If you talk too much and list too many reasons why you think you're right, you'll tax the patience of your staff. They will tune out and dismiss you as a lecturing blowhard. On the other hand, if you fail to give three solid points, they may remain skeptical, drill holes in your argument, or perhaps just walk away without committing to your position.

Most new managers find it easy to think in threes. The hard part is stopping once they're on a roll! You need to keep quiet after you deliver your trio of points. If you ramble or repeat yourself, then you'll lose your employees' attention.

Here are some ways to package your points in threes:

- Let's study this in three ways.
- Let's consider the three strongest reasons to go ahead with this.
- There are three factors driving this decision.
- There's a three-prong test we can apply to this problem.
- The three most important things to remember are . . .

When instructing or coaching your employees, a handy way to communicate with them is to speak in terms of problem-cause-solution. Begin by saying, "We need to confront this problem, find its cause, and propose solutions." Then proceed to walk them through each of the three stages, posing questions and giving guidance as needed.

A similar way to package your ideas in threes is to discuss facts-analysis-recommendation. Introduce your employees to the key facts that they must absorb in order to make headway. Then prod them to analyze the significance of the facts. Your goal is to help them answer the questions "What does all this mean?" and "What are the consequences?" Wrap up by inviting them to make suggestions or formal recommendations that flow from their analysis.

Pruning the Deadwood

Many new managers undergo a rite of passage that I call the Nervous Nellie phase. They are afraid to assert their authority or speak their mind. Until they get accustomed to their role, they're riddled with doubt or uncertainty whenever they answer their staff's questions or try to teach or discipline them. It's not a pretty sight.

In keeping with the spirit of the previous section, here are three ways to tell if you're a Nervous Nellie:

1. **You overdose on qualifiers.** Rookie managers often hesitate to commit to even the most simple statements. Instead of declaring, "This old customer relationship management software has to go," they say, "Maybe this old CRM software should be replaced." They qualify their remarks with words such as *perhaps, maybe,* and *generally.* While that's fine if you're a lawyer who must choose every word with precision, it can weaken your stature if you're a new manager struggling to prove yourself to your staff.

2. **You repeat yourself.** If you're anxious, you may rehash your point so much that your employees get tired of nodding their heads. If you assume that you need to make yourself abundantly clear, then you may insist on repeating or rephrasing basic instructions or observations ad nauseam.

3. **You ramble.** One reason to think in threes is it helps you stay on track. If you plunge right in and lecture to your staff or pontificate, you may ramble aimlessly. You'll jump from topic to topic randomly, leaving your listeners bewildered. They won't retain what you say, regardless of how many valid points you make. That's because you'll make it too hard for them to separate the wheat from the chaff.

Accept that you'll be nervous in your first days or weeks as a new manager. Like a jittery public speaker, however, you must ensure that your butterflies fly in formation. That means transforming your anxiety into positive energy.

AND NOW THE NEWS ...

FOR EXAMPLE

Barry took over a transaction processing unit at a bank. At first, he would pummel his staff into submission with his long-winded comments. They would avoid encounters for fear of hearing him babble at will. When Barry told me he used to work as a night copyeditor for his local newspaper and write headlines such as "Cubs Beat Mets" and "Peace Talks Put on Hold," I seized on that to coach him to improve as a manager. I said, "Talk to your staff the way you wrote headlines: subject, verb, object. Then stop talking and let them respond."

As a manager, you need to communicate with clarity and force. Less is more. By pruning the deadwood and sticking to the core message, you make it easier for your employees to understand you. Better yet, you leave more time for them to respond. As Lyndon Johnson said, "You can't learn nothin' if you're talkin'."

To prevent your anxiety from turning you into a motormouth, treat your words as a precious resource. Don't feel compelled to repeat yourself or add example after example. After you complete an important sentence, pause and give everyone a chance to reflect. Let a few seconds pass and see if anyone jumps in. Beware of speaking like a steamroller that flattens everything in its path.

Don't feel a need to inflate the importance of what you're saying. Keep your comments short and sweet; then engage employees in a give-and-take. This enables you to win their respect while training them to listen to your every word. They won't tune out if they know you're not likely to repeat yourself.

Avoid rambling; instead, tell anecdotes that drive home a simple but powerful point. Make sure each sentence advances the story so that you complete it in less than one minute. Beware of overexplaining or providing extraneous information that detracts from your main message.

Another way to speak succinctly is to give one-sentence contrasts. Examples include "Let's contrast what'll happen with or without the client's signed contract" or "Let's look at how we'd fare in the marketplace with or without the new branding campaign."

Crystallize your message by framing it in stark terms: either-or constructs, numbered lists (preferably three!), or compare-and-contrast. Structuring your comments in an orderly way keeps you from straying and inserting needless adverbs or fillers that can muddy your point.

SMART

MANAGING

THE 80/20 RULE

To avoid wasting words, strive to limit your speaking to 20 percent of the time and listen to your staffers the remaining 80 percent of the conversation. This applies primarily when you're trying to persuade, although it's a useful benchmark for most types of everyday encounters. Exception: When you want to explain a complex procedure or inform your staff of many new developments, then you may need to speak more than one-fifth of the time.

Loading up on words such as *frankly* and *extraordinarily* is like feeding your audience too much dessert. They're stuffed. They shut down because they've depleted too much energy digesting what you've said.

Your staff doesn't need to hear you carry on. Whether you're nervous or self-centered, your best bet is to cut your remarks to the bone.

Asking the Right Questions

There's an art to posing questions. By choosing the proper phrasing and speaking in a genuinely curious, inquisitive tone, you act as a true leader who helps employees discover lessons for themselves.

New managers often hesitate to ask questions under the mistaken impression that they're supposed to have all the answers. They may assume that admitting they don't know something is akin to showing a weakness.

"I figured when I became a manager that I would tell people what to do and, if necessary, how to do it," admitted a marketing manager after a year in the job. "It took me awhile to realize that my people hated being told what to do. They want me to help them, but not to strip away their dignity and their ability to think for themselves."

When you ask questions, you show your employees that you respect their ideas and opinions. You're letting them know that while you're their manager, you're not the fount of all wisdom. You want to learn from them, and you're willing to invest the time to hear what they have to say.

Better yet, you enhance your stature as a leader worth listening to. As a result of all your questions, you can then render judgments or issue orders that the troops will more readily respect. You can preface your conclusions by saying, "thanks to all of your input, ... " or "You've all taken a lot of time helping me understand this, and I'm grateful. Now I've decided ... "

A Gentle Prod — TRICKS OF THE TRADE

When your employees share insights with you or express their opinions, use three questions to push them to think for themselves and apply critical reasoning skills: "What's the significance of that?" "Is there anything you want to add?" "What do you conclude from that?" Your line of inquiry will guide them to examine an issue thoroughly and arrive at an action plan.

Like any communication skill, questioning can backfire if misused. If you reel off a series of accusatory or loaded questions such as "You didn't do what I asked, did you?" or "What are you not telling me?" or "Did it occur to you that there's more to it than that?," you invite scorn. Interrogate employees and you will alienate them. Posing questions dripping with dismay or disapproval will stir their resentment.

Consider the negativity behind the question, "Why didn't you tell me that would take so long?" Most employees will instantly defend themselves; they'll explain all that went wrong (and possibly how *you* contributed to the mess) to prove they're blameless. Meanwhile, you've lost a chance to build rapport. A less hostile question such as "How did you approach this project?" or "What steps did you take?" can help you understand why something took "so long" yet maintain a pleasant, nonthreatening dialogue with your employee.

Always maintain eye contact with your employee when you ask a question. Don't fidget, read, or eat. If you try to do two things at once, that makes others think that you're not giving your undivided attention to their answer.

I Care ... Really

CAUTION

Don't use questions because you think you should show interest—even when you don't really care. If you aren't curious to hear the answer, then keep quiet. An employee can sense when you're going through the motions. Your questions will lose their meaning, and you'll appear visibly distracted. Result: you've now done more damage than if you never asked the question at all.

Earlier in the chapter, we discussed the importance of pruning the deadwood so that you don't talk too much. Same goes when you question others. Keep your inquiries to one sentence. Never lace a question with lots of editorial comments or asides that test the patience of your employees. Come right out and ask what you want to know—and then stop talking!

Whenever you ask a question, stop immediately afterward. Purse your lips shut and await a response. If you're greeted with a few seconds of silence, don't fret. Some employees want an extra few moments to think before they talk. You should indulge them. Never jump in to repeat or rephrase the question, unless about seven seconds have passed and you're unsure whether the person heard you. Seven seconds will seem like an eternity, but it's enough time for almost anyone to gather their thoughts and at least take a stab at giving you an answer. (This holds true whether you're on the phone or speaking in person.)

> **Drowning question** A question that drowns the listener in verbiage. Rather than pose a simple, one-sentence question, you toss in lots of extra questions, side comments, and even answers to your own questions. The result: a confused employee who's unsure where to begin when you finally finish.
>
> **KEY TERM**

Make Your Words Sink In

When Tracy, the newly appointed leader of a software engineering unit, instructed her employee to learn a new operating system, she kept saying, "Don't do that" or "That won't work." Then she would demonstrate the "right" way to proceed.

As you might expect, Tracy's employee didn't feel great about the training session. After a few minutes, it felt like all Tracy could say was "No, you're wrong." Instead, Tracy should have let her trainee experiment with the system while playing a less hands-on role. If her employee tried to bypass certain commands, for instance, Tracy could have said, "When I've done that, the system stalled. Let's see if that happens to you." This helps both parties learn together, and Tracy doesn't make her subordinate feel like an order taker.

To speak like a leader, avoid making remarks that threaten or demean others. Examples of poor communication styles include bluntly contradicting someone, habitually volunteering your opinion, or rashly judging

> ### WHY JUDGE?
> You're a manager, not a judge in a courtroom. It's not your job to render verdicts on everything you see and hear. In a fast-paced workplace, it's tempting to draw quick conclusions about others' actions—and express your views in e-mails or text messages. Instead of judging, think like a scientist and dig for information. Learn more, empathize with others, and consider the context of a situation. Withhold your rulings unless or until they're needed.
>
> **CAUTION**

others. New managers may not realize just how often they fall into one of these traps.

When you disagree with an employee, say so. But speak diplomatically. Use phrases such as "I understand what you're saying, and I have to disagree" or "That's one way to look at it, although my experience leads me to a different conclusion." Don't feel a need to elaborate or justify your position in detail. Instead, stop and let the employee respond. Launch a friendly conversation, remain attentive, and treat what you hear seriously. Never prejudge or dismiss outright what a staffer says.

To maximize the odds that your team retains what you're about to say, tie it to something they've already said. Play back the words they've used as a way to pry open their minds to accept your input. If you want them to buy into yet another round of budget cuts, begin by saying, "You're told me many times that you want ..." or "Remember at last week's meeting when you asked me ..." After you remind them of their past comments, connect your new message so that it fits right in.

FROM WHAT YOU'VE TOLD ME ...

FOR EXAMPLE

Will needed to prod one of his least committed employees to work harder. He had tried before, but the employee ultimately gave the same halfhearted effort. This time Will said, "You told me something the other day that stayed with me. You said that you're perfectly happy to be left alone, that you don't need much supervision. I'm happy to oblige, but you'll make it easier for me to leave you alone if you meet certain performance standards." By acknowledging his employee's preferences and proving how well he listened and retained what he was told, Will convinced this individual to improve.

To ensure your words sink in, never rush to give commands and then walk away. Employees resent a manager who barks orders at a rapid pace, only to cut the conversation short at a moment's notice. You'll leave your listeners bewildered and probably annoyed.

Try to reserve a few minutes to confirm that your staff understood your comments. Solicit their feedback with questions such as "Does this make sense?" or "Is there anything else you think we should consider?"

When sending a message on your smartphone or tablet PC, make requests in a friendly tone. Don't type "do this ASAP" or "no screwups!"

Inserting "please" and "thanks" won't assure that others will welcome your terse directives, but at least you lower the risk of coming across as a too-busy-to-care boss.

If you're on the phone, don't hang up until you get at least some acknowledgment that the other party heard you. Ideally, this happens when your employee summarizes your remarks or reviews what actions need to occur. To avoid misunderstandings, check that you made yourself clear by saying, "Tell me how you'll proceed from here."

By leaving time for others to respond, you can create a more comfortable give-and-take in which employees demonstrate that they paid attention to you. Rather than assume your words sunk in, you'll know beyond any doubt that your message reached its destination intact.

New Manager's Checklist for Chapter 5

☑ Pause frequently to avoid stringing words together. Project your voice clearly, especially when you're addressing a group.

☑ Think in threes. Prepare a trio of points that you want to make so that you give employees enough support to substantiate your views— without going overboard and talking too much.

☑ Avoid qualifiers that weaken your message or needlessly reveal your doubts.

☑ When you're trying to persuade an employee, limit your speaking to 20 percent of the time and listen the remaining 80 percent of the conversation. This ensures you'll treat your words as a precious resource.

☑ Avoid blatantly contradicting employees; instead, propose "another way of looking at it."

☑ To increase the odds that your staffers understand and retain what you say, tie your messages to what they've told you before.

The Art of Motivation

When a manager complains to me, "I wish I could motivate Gus," here's what he really means: "I wish I could get Gus to do his job better."

The whole point of trying to excite your employees is to make them more productive. The stronger their commitment to superior performance, the easier it becomes to motivate them. It's like preaching to the choir. Apathetic individuals probably won't respond to your motivational management because they don't *want* to do well; they're content to give a minimal effort and see no reason to push any harder.

New managers often assume that they're great motivators if they communicate enthusiastically and see changes in employees' behavior. But getting workers to pump their fists or act like cheerleaders won't matter much if they're not competent or reliable. That's why true motivation does more than modify an individual's behavior; it lifts the level of performance and produces a more valuable, driven employee.

Before we look at specific techniques, here are three basic rules of effective motivation:

1. Never ask others to do anything you wouldn't do yourself.
2. Flood employees with feedback. Don't wait for periodic performance reviews to let them know how they're doing.
3. Encourage them to talk with you about the good *and* bad aspects of

their job. If they complain on occasion, don't label them as malcontents and dismiss their comments. Listen and understand what bothers them before you judge.

Press the Right Buttons

Some medical schools now require their students to spend time as a patient in a hospital. They're told they have a certain disease, and it's their job to play the part. The hospital doesn't know they're really students. The experience of getting poked, probed, and pushed from room to room changes their outlook, and these students often claim to learn more from this exercise than from any textbook.

Just think what would happen if you could experience a day in the life of some of your employees. You would understand the pressures they face and the environment within which they operate. If you could arrange such a role reversal, you'd see close up what matters most to these employees. You would learn how they make decisions, handle adversity, and derive satisfaction from their work. And that would take the guesswork out of motivating them.

As a new manager, you can probably remember life as a worker bee. Perhaps you can identify with some of the anxieties and irritations that your current staff feels. Cling to these memories and keep them fresh. They will unlock your motivational skills.

Also realize that you there's no single secret to effective motivation. Everyone's different, so you'll need to tailor your approach for each employee.

More than ever, people crave meaning in their work. Younger individuals launching their careers want to make a difference, not just earn a paycheck. But some employees love the spotlight; they will do anything to garner public praise or win awards. Others dread such attention; they're embarrassed when they're singled out for their superior effort, performance, or results. Some people care less about praise and more about learning and developing their skills. They might even sacrifice higher pay in exchange for richer professional growth experiences.

Reach Out with Empathy

Employee motivation begins with empathy. When you can step into another person's shoes and appreciate their attitudes and concerns, you can then identify their priorities, values, and beliefs. Based on this awareness, you can isolate the hot-button issues that they care about most. This in turn enables you to appeal to them on their level. Your attempt to motivate becomes a bridge to build better mutual understanding.

The best way to empathize is to clear away all your biases and assumptions when you relate to others. Ask yourself, "If I were [name of your employee], what would matter most to me?" The more often you stop and chat with this person and listen attentively to his or her comments, the sooner you'll answer your question. Note what topics each employee raises with you; a surefire way to uncover people's hot buttons is to pay attention to their gripes, jokes, and requests.

TELL ME MORE

TRICKS OF THE TRADE

To properly motivate people, get to know them first and empathize. Ask frequent questions such as, "Are you happy with your progress?" or "Are you pleased with your office?" or "How would you rate the type of work you're doing?" Don't settle for neutral or noncommittal answers. Prod them to reveal more. After about a dozen of these conversations, you'll start to notice recurring subjects that each employee tends to raise, ranging from concern over lack of teamwork to disappointment with the company's policies and procedures. This tells you what they care about most; use this information to motivate more effectively.

Motivation is not a spectator sport. You can't empathize with people from afar, and you can't delegate this task to others. There's no way to step into someone else's shoes unless you invest time in getting to know them. If you drop in on an employee once every few months, say "great job," rush off in a flash, and assume you've worked some kind of motivational magic, guess again. Such a hurried display can actually do more harm than good, because it makes people feel unimportant.

The best way to motivate is eyeball-to-eyeball. Devote time to talk with people. Reward them with your presence; that alone will help you build the kind of camaraderie that will lead to a more energized workforce.

NO REWARDS, NO ENGAGEMENT

One of the most powerful ways to motivate people is to promise to promote them for top performance—or at least bestow meaningful rewards when they excel. Yet in a 2012 survey of U.S. federal workers, only 43 percent said their employers provide performance awards or job advancement opportunities. Federal staffers with lower-paid jobs were even less satisfied with performance-based awards than higher-paid individuals, leaving managers seeking new ways to reward people at low rungs of the ladder.

TOOLS

In the twenty-first-century workplace, managers and employees are less likely to work under the same roof. It's hard to establish eye contact with a staffer who's 500 miles away. While mobile technology has revolutionized how we communicate, it presents a downside for new managers trying to motivate their far-flung team.

Gallup, a research firm, takes an annual poll of companies to gauge employee attitudes. Over the last decade, Gallup's data has revealed that over two-thirds of workers at U.S. firms are not motivated to perform productively. Specifically, the findings indicate that most employees are "not engaged" or "actively disengaged."

Engaged employees share their employer's values and care about its mission. They feel pride—not shame—about their organization's products or services. They are more apt to refer friends to work for their employer and urge others to buy what it sells.

Even if you don't see all your employees daily, make every effort to connect with them as fully dimensional people. Show interest in them. Retain personal tidbits that they share with you. Ask how you can support their success. While these steps won't assure a high level of engagement, they go a long way toward establishing your presence as a trusted leader.

Isolate the Need

In order to press the right buttons, you must know what to look for. All employees are different, but you can still generalize about what motivates them.

Prior to the rash of downsizings that began in December 2007 (the official start of the Great Recession), many employees craved safety and security. But that all changed as the economy sputtered. By mid-2010, a

Pew Research study found that 55 percent of adults in the U.S. workforce sustained hardship of some kind (such as job loss, pay cut, or reduction in hours). Motivators from the twentieth century—from job security to reliably generous pensions—now seem quaint.

Today's workers are altogether tougher and more complex. Few employees expect a job to insulate them from harsh elements and threats of the unknown; issues of safety and security rarely matter as much in this fluid, rapidly changing economy. Instead, most people are motivated by one of these six needs: attainment, power, belonging, independence, respect, and equity.

In your first few months as a manager, you may have trouble determining which one of these six hot buttons applies to each of your subordinates. Here's how you can tell:

Attainment. Some employees love the act of achieving something. They want to sharpen their skills to reach greater heights, and they're pleased if you can give them assignments that force them to stretch a bit and overcome considerable challenges. You can spot these employees by their goal-driven determination and their willingness to ignore office politics in favor of sinking their teeth into a project that tests their talents and harnesses their skills. Motivate them by constantly introducing new tasks that build on each other. Allow them to meet both short- and long-term goals, thus creating a pipeline of achievement that's theirs for the taking.

Power. Rather than live for attainment, some individuals thrive on exerting influence and control. They like the feeling of importance that comes from calling the shots. These employees usually try to hog center stage at meetings and state bold, controversial opinions. They also may draw attention to themselves with their high-visibility stabs at leadership,

> **MAKING PROGRESS**
> **FOR EXAMPLE**
>
> The top motivator for many professionals is moving forward on meaningful projects, according to research by Teresa Amabile at Harvard Business School. Coauthor of *The Progress Principle* (Harvard Business Press, 2011), she found that employees' "best days" occurred when they made progress on projects viewed as meaningful to the organization's mission. To motivate employees to enjoy "best days," assign tasks that advance your team toward key goals.

such as volunteering to serve as team spokesperson. This type of individual may buttonhole the chief executive officer at a party and curry favor with high-level consultants and other outsiders who radiate power and authority. Treat these employees like in-house experts and frequently ask them for advice. This will motivate them because they'll savor the chance to offer their opinions and see that you take them seriously.

Belonging. Employees who want to feel a sense of comradeship are among the easiest to motivate: Just leave them alone to build rapport with their coworkers. Make sure they have plenty of chances to get to know their colleagues in informal settings, such as company picnics and other outings that occur outside of the normal workday. Because these individuals find the social aspects of their job the most meaningful, you can motivate them by making them feel like they're part of a larger group. For example, arrange meetings where they can collaborate and share ideas, rather than sit and listen to lectures or formal presentations. Satisfy their need for affiliation, and they'll give you a solid effort.

Independence. Some employees seek autonomy above all else. They want the freedom to experiment with their job assignments and function at least somewhat independently. If you micromanage their every move, you'll deaden their desire to go the extra mile. You'll know you're managing independent workers if they chafe whenever you enact new policies or procedures. They will reject new rules and rebel against bossy supervisors. The best way to motivate these freedom seekers is to give them overriding goals and let them find the best way to produce results. Without showing favoritism, try giving them the flexibility to set their own hours, make unhindered choices, and decide what steps they want to take to get the job done.

Respect. Like comedian Rodney Dangerfield, some employees simply want a little respect. These individuals may storm out of a room if they feel ignored or "dissed." They also may follow rules of office etiquette to the extreme, dressing conservatively in well-pressed clothes and cultivating an almost military bearing. You can motivate them by listening to them. Nod and give them full eye contact when they talk. Avoid checking your computer or smartphone while they're speaking to you. Don't interrupt them or shake your head in disagreement as soon as they open their

mouth. Lavish them with recognition and feedback on their performance, especially praise. While you should apply these tips whenever you
manage, it's particularly important when you're trying to fulfill an
employee's need for esteem.

Equity. While everyone likes to work for a fair, unbiased boss, some
employees see the world almost exclusively through the eyes of just versus
unjust. They may compare how you manage your staff's work schedules,
job titles, scope of responsibilities, pay, and benefits to ensure there are no
hints of inequities. They take it upon themselves to police your authority.
They will not hesitate to tell you if they think something's unfair, and
they'll eagerly point out inconsistencies in your management style and
decision making. Motivate these workers by thinking like an employment
lawyer. Give them objective evidence to prove that you're a fair, equitable
boss. For example, distribute industry-wide salary surveys to show these
employees how you arrived at pay scales, and explain how compensation
relates to job grade or job description. Tell them you will not tolerate any
hint of bias or impropriety. Encourage them to let you know if they detect
even a perceived inequity so that you have a chance to correct it.

CREATE AN "APPRECIATION BOARD"

SMART

When employees want to express appreciation to a coworker for
superior effort or performance, ask them to write their comments and give them to the recipient. At Legal Monkeys, a Texas-
based legal services firm, employees write with a dry-erase
MANAGING
marker on an 8x10 framed glass board. They give the board to the colleague whom they appreciate, who proudly keeps it until he or she erases
the note, writes a new one, and passes it on to a deserving coworker. Getting employees in the habit of praising each other lifts everyone's spirits
and creates a self-perpetuating positive culture.

Moving Beyond Money

Many new managers assume motivation is a breeze. They figure as long
as they can throw money at people, they'll perform like trained seals.

While cash certainly counts for most of us, it's overrated as a motivational tool. It's the lifeblood of business, but it doesn't necessarily drive
every employee to excel or even to care.

"I've learned you motivate people by treating them like you want to be treated," Richard Jenrette told me. Jenrette, the cofounder of the Wall Street firm Donaldson, Lufkin & Jenrette, is also the retired chairman and CEO of The Equitable Companies, an insurance firm. "Money alone won't do it. Let me give you an example. I just met with a talented guy who got a $30 million bonus from a big Wall Street brokerage firm. But then he quit. Why? Because no one called him to congratulate him. A check just showed up with no note, nothing. 'I figured they didn't care,' he said. He lost the motivation to work there because he felt no one noticed him."

Same goes if you seek to extract extra time and effort from your already overworked team. Don't dangle cash rewards and conclude that's all the motivation they'll need. Instead, appeal to their sense of pride and responsibility for a job well done.

Give employees ways to exert control or influence over their work. Most people have a psychological need to shape their daily lives, rather than react helplessly as crises pelt them from all sides. You'll not only motivate your staff but also cut their stress level by respecting their ability to call at least some of the shots.

MISTAKE PROOFING

MORE MONEY, MORE MONEY

You load up on gift cards for retailers or restaurants and give them out whenever you see someone excel on the job. Nice idea, except it probably won't motivate. Employees can come to expect cash bonuses and resent it when they give full effort and don't receive something extra. Instead of cash, consider flexible schedules as a motivator. A 2012 survey by Accenture found that 64 percent of employees stayed put because their job offered flexibility to, say, work from home or set their own hours.

Another strategy to motivate without money is to show how you intend to track your employees' work product. As seasoned managers often like to say, "What you measure is what you get." For instance, if you want to rally your troops to double-check their work before turning it in, say, "I'll be tracking your reports and recognizing those employees who do error-free work." Then follow through and publicly praise those individuals who consistently produce work without mistakes.

"As a manager, what you do is two times as important as what you say when you want to motivate your employees," said Don Harrison, founder and president of Implementation Management Associates, a consulting firm in Lakewood, Colorado. "And what you reinforce is three times as important as what you say. Managers underestimate the amount of scrutiny they're under by their employees, so they need to constantly reinforce that they want to send a clear message to their employees."

Strive to tie an individual's hard work to a meaningful, concrete result. If you want to motivate your team to enact a new procedure, tell them that their compliance will help the company reduce its paper usage by 7 percent and cut its administrative expenses by 10 percent over the next year. The fact that they can make a difference in the bottom line can serve as sufficient motivation in itself. Help your staff equate their effort with something real, as opposed to saying, "Do this and you'll be a hero."

Recognition is free. Salute the genuinely fine work of your employees, and you're assured of motivating them. Express praise in public and private. Never fear you'll overdo it, as long as you can honestly express admiration or gratitude. No amount of money can make a worker feel as elated as a manager who takes the time to smile and say, "Your contribution to this project was absolutely invaluable" or "You set such a great example of what I'm looking for here. Great job."

Let's say you empathize with your employees and you conclude that they're eager to advance in your organization. Ambitious people may want more than your recognition. Introduce them to senior management and invite them to join you in high-level meetings or conferences where they will meet influential executives. Establish cross-departmental teams and motivate your star employees by selecting them to participate.

LET'S EAT OUT!

Guy and Susan Sylvester run a 19-employee environmental services firm in Portsmouth, New Hampshire. Every year, they take each of their employees out to eat to discuss career development. The staffer picks the restaurant (some choose a fancy steakhouse, others opt for their favorite breakfast diner). Guy and Susan ask, "What do you want to be doing in three or five years?" and "How can we help you get there?" The meal doubles as a motivational session: employees feel more valued and appreciate working for business owners who invest in their professional growth.

Reconfigure their job duties so that they can gain responsibility and experience in areas that interest them.

A great motivational technique is to treat employees' ideas seriously and respond promptly to their sensible proposals and valid complaints. Whether you set up an online suggestion box or keep an open-door policy and hear them out, do not ignore their input. Following up quickly will motivate them to try harder and feel better about you and the whole organization.

Knowledge: The Ultimate Motivator

While there's no foolproof motivator that will instantly transform every one of your staffers into hard-charging superstars, you can bet that they will almost all respond well to the gift of knowledge. Give people the chance to learn and grow both personally and professionally, and they will invest more of themselves in the job.

Dangle training and advancement opportunities as rewards for fine work. Select your most diligent or outstanding employees to attend outside seminars and conferences where they can expand their network, pick up new skills, and return to work with fresh perspectives. Sit down for 30 minutes with a high-potential newcomer and show how to master a tough task, leaving time for the worker to demonstrate the new skill. Make your office a place where everyone shares insights freely and collaborates to find better ways to work.

At Cognizant Technology Solutions, a Teaneck, New Jersey–based global information technology provider with more than 145,000 employees worldwide, managers motivate people by encouraging them to pool their knowhow. The company uses a "wiki"—an internal web portal—for employees to share knowledge and best practices with each other. Through this online platform, they can seek help from in-house technical experts or discuss lessons learned in handling client accounts.

The fact that most Cognizant employees are under age 30 makes this kind of resource especially popular. Because younger individuals grew up using social media, they feel comfortable tapping their coworkers' collective intelligence via crowdsourcing and other forms of online outreach.

Regardless of the average age of your employees, you can offer collaborative, knowledge-sharing platforms that harness the Internet to bring people together. Make it easy for workers to "talk" with each other across departments or across borders. Most individuals spend a huge amount of time online, so help them search for information they need from colleagues who possess it.

WELCOME TO THE ROUNDTABLE

Create a new tradition at your company called a *roundtable*. This consists of an informal monthly meeting of about 10 employees with a top executive from your company. The purpose: to help the employees learn about the organization's most recent financial per- **TOOLS** formance, such as the latest quarterly results. Encourage participants to ask questions about operations and bottom-line concerns. Invite a mix of attendees that includes a few managers along with lower-level workers from other departments. This way, these sessions can also serve as a way for employees in different parts of the company (and at different levels) to mingle.

While we've already warned you that money isn't necessarily the only or best way to motivate people, helping employees learn how the organization makes it can produce a big payoff. The more you can demystify the innards of the business and help your workers track the cash flow throughout the company, the more they'll tie their job to the firm's larger bottom-line performance. In fact, 59 percent of employees in an Ernst & Young survey said the best way to motivate them is for their managers to teach them how their jobs help the company make money. And 77 percent of the managers in the same survey agreed.

In the 1990s, the notion of "open-book management" caught fire as a motivational tool. By educating employees to understand your department's and the organization's budgets and income statements, you can show them the link between their jobs and the organization's larger success. That can

Open-book management
Educating your employees in the bottom-line operations of your organization   **KEY TERM**
by opening the books or teaching them how to read the financial information that the senior executives track.

in turn prod them to work smarter and rededicate themselves to operating productively.

To implement an open-book approach, begin by identifying a key number that you and your bosses use to measure your unit's performance.

In insurance, loss ratios reveal to what extent the business is profitable. Airlines look at load factor (number of seats filled). Banks, mortgage servicing firms, and credit card issuers track delinquencies or default rates. As a new manager, you should find out what figures matter most to higher-ups and make it your business to follow these numbers with keen interest.

The next step to motivate employees is not only to tell them what numbers you're watching, but to explain the cash-flow process, the difference between revenue and profit, and how to read an income statement and balance sheet. If you're not already familiar with these concepts, spend a few hours with your boss to learn what you need to know.

Finally, establish a clear "line of sight" for employees to connect their jobs to bottom-line benchmarks. A sales assistant who responds to customer inquiries may soon appreciate the importance of speed in replying to client e-mails. Through open-book discussions, sales assistants can better connect quick responses to customers with client retention, which in turn might reduce the company's spending on costly marketing campaigns to attract new customers.

> **TRICKS OF THE TRADE**
>
> ## MAKE IT EASY TO KEEP SCORE
>
> To motivate your employees to monitor bottom-line numbers, create an easy-to-read scorecard so that everyone can see how they're contributing to a quantifiable organizational goal. Examples include a weekly e-mail update on administrative expenses, profits per employee, or sales growth. By releasing new numbers on an ongoing basis, you can rivet the team's attention on how they can make a difference in the company's performance.

Motivating the "Unmotivatable"

You've tried everything. Now you're ready to give up.

Some employees just don't seem to respond to anything. You can compliment them profusely, give them a generous raise, promote them, or simply leave them alone to do their work. Whatever motivational strategy you try, you get the same result: a drone who treads water and gives a 70 or 80 percent effort—enough to meet all job requirements but not nearly sufficient if you want to manage a winning team of exceptional, high-producing superstars.

You may be tempted to shrug and say, "I can't figure out how to motivate this person, so I'll focus on others." But before you conclude there's nothing else you can do, reconsider the steps you've taken so far. Chances are, you've tried to motivate by relying on the 3Ps: pay, praise, and promises (of advance-

WATCH YOUR MOUTH

CAUTION

When you have trouble motivating an employee, don't publicize it. Rookie managers may vent their frustration by telling coworkers, "I just can't crack that nut" or "I've tried everything, and I guess he's just burned out." When you volunteer such opinions and talk behind the employee's back, you risk alienating him or her further.

ment, more money, more responsibility, etc.). That's not going to work for the toughest 5 percent of your employees who won't respond to the same carrots that appeal to most others. You need to dig deeper.

To solve the puzzle of motivating apathetic employees, resort to more creative measures. Promising advancement won't work, because she has probably topped out and she knows it. Promising money won't work, because she has pushed her salary grade to its absolute limit, and she lacks the skills or credentials to move up. Promising accomplishment or power won't work, because she no longer cares about leaving her mark or exerting her influence.

Try introducing change into the employee's routine. Have her jettison her normal duties and devote more time to challenging projects that harness her expertise. Explain that with her talent, she's an ideal candidate to

A PICTURE SPEAKS 1,000 WORDS

FOR EXAMPLE

Mindy wanted to motivate Steve to regain his momentum as a top salesperson after a prolonged slump. Steve didn't respond to anything: incentive trips, bonuses, the corner office. When Mindy met with him to review yet another dismal month's production, she brought along some old photos of Steve winning company-wide awards at an annual banquet, including the president shaking his hand and a beaming Steve waving from the stage to hundreds of his wildly applauding coworkers. Mindy didn't say much; she just let Steve gaze at the photos. The memories they evoked made Steve reassess his current malaise and rededicate himself to bouncing back.

make a more significant or lasting contribution to the organization. Add that your unit's success depends on her ability to "give 100 percent."

I met a new manager who motivated a 20-year veteran by saying, "You know, I hate waste—any waste. I don't waste money. I leave a clean plate after every meal. I always recycle. As I see it, you're this gem who's not shining as much anymore. I can't stand to see so much talent go to waste."

The manager worked with the employee to rearrange his job so that he could train newcomers and serve as a kind of in-house consultant. This strategy not only gave the employee a fresh outlook, but it made him dread the idea of squandering his ability and further upsetting his manager.

If the employee once produced better results, appeal to pride. Don't dwell on past glories, but show how much better the present and future can turn out. Like a psychic looking into a crystal ball, describe in exciting detail how the employee's actions today can lead to undeniably huge rewards in the future.

New Manager's Checklist for Chapter 6

☑ Never ask an employee to do something that you wouldn't do yourself.

☑ Use empathy to uncover your employees' hot buttons. Ask lots of questions and dig for clues for what makes them tick.

☑ Motivate by measuring performance and praising those who exceed objectives.

☑ Give employees responsibility and listen to their ideas, which encourages them to treat their jobs more seriously.

☑ Teach your team to link their jobs to the bottom line. Apply "open-book management" techniques so that they can examine the same numbers that you and your bosses do.

☑ Motivate the "unmotivatables" by assigning them special projects and allowing them to teach and train others in their area of expertise.

Dishing Out Criticism

t's your first few weeks as manager, and you're already confronting people problems. You've inherited an employee who seems predisposed to crack nasty jokes at meetings instead of communicating in a civil tone. Another staffer can't stop complaining about the new software that you "forced everyone" to install. Finally, a loudmouth billing specialist stomps around all day radiating such anger that you're concerned a fight will break out.

All these employees need constructive criticism from you. Yes, *criticism*. If that word sounds harsh, get used to it. A big part of your new job as manager is to let your workers know what they're doing wrong and how they can improve.

Let's clear up something right off the bat: you want to be liked by your employees. You've always dreaded supervisors who judged you relentlessly and who found fault with your every move. You vowed that when *you* became a manager, you would lay off the incessant criticism to avoid hurting your employees.

Nice idea. But the cold, hard truth is you must criticize your staff—often. Keeping quiet and hoping problems go away on their own rarely works. In fact, by refusing to tell people what they're doing wrong, you perpetuate a destructive status quo. Employees continue to falter, and the price of their poor performance or behavior inevitably soars.

You may fear that criticism will unleash negative or self-defeating feelings among subordinates and that their morale will plummet. That will only happen if you criticize thoughtlessly. You will learn in this chapter that if you express yourself clearly and diplomatically, you need not leave lasting scars.

At the other extreme, you may fear for your own hide if you dare criticize a strong-willed, sharp-tongued veteran. Some new managers tell me they are intimidated by their most vocal, opinionated, and charismatic employees. It's that much harder to give negative feedback to someone who seems unwilling or unable to listen to management.

As you read the techniques that follow, remember that your employees expect to get feedback from you. They know they're not perfect, and they know that as the boss it's your job to point out ways for them to do better. As much as you may not like to criticize, realize that it's a skill like negotiating or public speaking. The more you do it, the easier it becomes.

SMART MANAGING

SHOULD I KEEP QUIET?
When you're weighing whether to criticize an employee, follow this procedure: imagine it's six months later and you haven't said a word. What's the worst that can happen? If an individual's bad habits or unacceptable attitude can wreak havoc on your unit, then you may conclude it's smarter to act now than to keep quiet. But if taking the long view helps you realize the issue is relatively minor and may take care of itself, then perhaps you can let yourself off the hook and not criticize.

Younger workers are particularly eager to receive feedback. They may demand input on an almost daily basis, driving you crazy (even if you're their age—or younger—and you identify with their thirst for feedback).

Rather than wait for the annual review, consider conducting mini-reviews every quarter. They'll still want more, but at least you'll set a reasonable expectation for supplying ongoing critiques of their performance.

To increase the amount of constructive criticism that flows among your team, arrange for peer-to-peer feedback mechanisms. That way, you signal that it's everyone's job to offer helpful input to everyone else.

Online resources make this easy. Using www.work.com or www .coworkers.com, you can set up ongoing feedback systems for employees to comment on their colleagues' performance. These web-based social tools function best if your organizational culture revolves around openness and supportive coaching. In less trustful or highly politicized work environments, peer feedback can degenerate into sniping or settling scores.

Focus on Performance, Not Personality

This chapter opened with examples of three employees who cry out for criticism. It would be easy to say to them, "Your tasteless jokes aren't appropriate" or "Stop complaining" or "You look so angry today." Easy, but wrong.

The right way to criticize is to focus on *observable* actions, not attitudes. Instead of saying, "Your jokes are inappropriate," say, "When Eleanor suggested a new formula for computing the value of these accounts, your response about her 'dumb math' was inappropriate." And rather than say, "You look so angry today," say, "Why did you snarl and speak so loudly to that temp?"

By limiting your criticism to what you can see with your own eyes, you refrain from judgments that can trigger the defensive reflex (see Chapter 4). Most people will instinctively defend themselves if you attack their personality or deliver unfair or inflated criticism that moves beyond what's measurable or observable.

Consider the last time you criticized an employee. One measure of your success is whether you were interrupted. If your staffer seemed to listen and let you finish, then that's a small victory. At least you didn't tick off the other person from the moment you opened your mouth. But if the person cut you off and started defending, denying, or otherwise punching holes in your comments,

> ### STOP BEFORE YOU GET PERSONAL
> **FOR EXAMPLE**
>
> During the U.S. Senate confirmation hearing on Lawrence Summers's nomination to be Treasury secretary, a senator recalled angrily that Summers once criticized politicians who want to cut estate taxes as motivated by selfishness. "What I said was wrong," Summers admitted to the Senate. "It's never a good idea in policy debates to impugn motives." That's a wise lesson for new managers, too. If you're going to criticize, stick to the facts so that you don't get personal.

AVOID THE "WORST" WORDS

The three most dangerous words to use when you're dishing out criticism are *always*, *never*, and *worst*. If you let slip any of these words, you're overstating your case and assigning blame rather than focusing on actual performance. "You always do that" or "I've never seen you do this right" are guaranteed to engender ill will. By limiting your criticism to observable actions, you'll wind up saying, "You did that three times this week" or "I've seen you do this incorrectly at least a dozen times since we started processing the business this way."

you may want to rethink your choice of words.

Another example of poor wording is to follow the word *you* with a negative. For instance, saying, "You didn't do that the way I asked" or "You won't listen to reason" will inflame tensions and leave employees feeling shaken and resentful. New managers who are unaccustomed to criticizing subordinates often wind up sounding accusatory when they're trying to assert their authority.

You'll talk your way into trouble by making sweeping generalizations or value judgments when you criticize. One reason to describe actions and performance rather than intangibles such as attitude and personality traits is that you'll steer clear of the gross exaggerations that come with sloppy criticism. You'll know you're on shaky ground if you overuse the words *is* and *are* (as in "Gene, you are wrong").

In mathematics, *is* means *equals* (i.e., two plus two is four). That's why it pays to avoid *is* and *are* when you criticize; otherwise, you wind up equating the person with an undesirable characteristic. And that's a sure sign you're discussing personality rather than concrete performance issues.

Descriptions Versus Inferences

With all these warnings about words to avoid when you're criticizing employees, you may figure it's almost impossible to say anything safe that will sound supportive and nonthreatening. Actually, it's easy to level with someone in a fair, unbiased tone: just say what you see.

When you describe what you can see, your eyes become cameras. You're taking snapshots of your employees' actions. Your words paint an image that's crisp, clear, and true, free from ambiguities, interpretations, or exaggerations. Better yet, you ensure that your criticism flows from solid empirical evidence rather than vague or biased accusations.

You may be thinking, "Of course I describe behavior when I criticize. There's no other way to do it." But a trap awaits those who confuse descriptions with inferences.

Words such as *careless, temperamental, lazy, self-righteous, arrogant,* and *sloppy* do not reveal anything about an individual's actions, only what can be inferred. Managers who lack precise communication skills may rely on these judgment-laden words when they criticize while failing to substantiate their views.

Inferences Judgments that do not report actual events, behaviors, or actions, but what you can **KEY TERM** infer from them. Inferences allow you to jump from one statement that you consider true to another that's supposedly true, but careful listeners may reject your reasoning.

Let's take three examples. If you witnessed an employee get into three arguments today, that's a description you may want to share with that individual. But if you say, "Boy, you're belligerent today," such an inference will probably lead to yet another argument!

TEST YOURSELF   **TRICKS OF THE TRADE**

How can you tell the difference between descriptions and inferences? Before you criticize, ask yourself, "What is this employee doing?" Your answer must describe observable behavior and give a specific, detailed account of events or actions. If you lack evidence or cannot say what you've seen with your own eyes, don't rush to criticize.

Similarly, if you say, "I've seen you walk down the hall with your head down, refuse to say hello to anyone, and repeatedly give only the barest one-word answers to customers' questions," that's better than saying, "You seem down, and your moodiness concerns me." And if you notice an employee returning from a two-hour lunch break, you may label that person "irresponsible" or "slacking off."

By describing what you see, however, you avoid making inferences that may prove wrong. If you approach the late-arriving employee and say, "You left for lunch two hours ago, right?" you may learn that his late return was caused by a serious accident. If you say, "I've heard you get

CAUTION

DESCRIPTIONS CAN STILL STING

Descriptions are clear, but not necessarily more pleasant than inferences. Even if you say what you see, your employees might guess what inferences you're drawing and feel angry or threatened. Nevertheless, it's safer and smarter to refrain from judgments and simply report what actions you observed.

into three arguments today," you may learn that your employee isn't belligerent as much as passionate about supporting the company's objectives.

Descriptions and inferences can work together when you want to give feedback. If you're still getting to know your new employees, don't assume they can figure out what conclusion you're drawing when you merely say what you see. You may want to lead with a description and then follow up with an inference.

Let's say you tell one of your clerks, "Earlier today you took work from Ron's desk and started processing it when you finished going through your work." That statement alone doesn't mean much. Your employee will wonder, "Am I being criticized? Is the boss upset with me? What's going on?" You need to draw a conclusion to drill home your point.

"That's the kind of aggressiveness I like to see—good job in keeping busy!" shows your approval of this behavior.

"It's not right for you to snoop around someone else's desk and take things without their permission, even if your intentions are good" reveals that you're not entirely pleased.

Express Criticism as a Question

To make your criticism more palatable to employees, you may want to present it as a question and let them discover for themselves what's wrong. This tactic works especially well with high-ego performers who automatically resist any input they perceive as negative.

When John Calley ran Warner Bros. movie studio in the late 1970s, he had to tell writer/director Irwin Allen that his latest script, *The Walter Syndrome*, was terrible. But Calley knew Allen would not accept criticism. So when Allen said, "Take your best shot," Calley didn't go for the bait. Instead, he said, "Irwin, I wouldn't presume to talk story with you, because of who you are—because you are Irwin Allen. I am just not that brazen."

"I understand," Allen replied.

Calley said that instead he would like to ask one question.

"I can't say I'm not intrigued," Allen said. "What is the question?"

"My question is this. Would Cecil B. DeMille [an important movie producer of the era] have made *The Walter Syndrome*?"

At that moment, Allen dropped the script into the trash and declared it "a closed issue" (from *The New Yorker*, March 21, 1994, p. 82).

Calley's ability to ask a penetrating question saved him from having to criticize Allen's work. It helped Allen realize that his script wasn't worthy of one of the greatest moviemakers of the century—without Calley having to utter even one critical comment.

You can borrow Calley's shrewd technique when you're managing your staff, although in most cases you'll need to offer at least some description before you ask your question. Strive to couple a succinct descriptive comment with a fair, unbiased question.

CRITICIZE WITHOUT CRITICISM

When Mark's employee failed to meet a key deadline, Mark was tempted to say, "I never missed a deadline when I had your job. Now that I'm a manager, I'm not going to tolerate it when my staff can't deliver on time!" But Mark thought better of that aggressive approach. Instead, he used a one-two punch of a description followed by a question. "Last Friday, we agreed you would complete this task by today at 9:00 a.m. It's now noon. Can you explain why this happened and help me decide to what extent I should expect you to meet deadlines in the future?"

As a new manager, you may want to use role reversal as a way to avoid direct criticism of your employees. Here's how:

1. Schedule a private meeting in your office with your employee.
2. When the employee arrives, invite him to sit in your chair while you sit in the visitor's chair.
3. From your visitor's seat, ask, "What would you say if you were in my shoes, and I had to criticize you for what happened?"
4. Stay silent. Let the employee respond. Some subordinates will prove so rough in their self-criticism that you need not add a word.

A manager at a nonprofit agency successfully used this strategy when her aide, Gary, consistently arrived at work late and didn't respond to repeated requests to show up on time. She had Gary sit in her chair and asked him, "You know how much I need you here at 8:30 every morning. I've tried everything, but in the last week you haven't made it in on time once. What would you say if you were me?"

Gary tried to stall, hoping his boss would interrupt. She didn't. So he kept talking, firing off excuse after excuse. Finally, he started to feel embarrassed by his behavior. So he disciplined himself by saying, "I see there's no good excuse for such a lousy track record of coming in late. If I don't make it in at least 90 percent of the time over the next six months, I would have it affect my performance review and possibly jeopardize the promotion I'm shooting for."

Gary's hard-nosed response impressed his boss. His rough self-reprimand enabled her to make him aware of his unacceptable actions without lashing out at him.

Aside from reducing the amount of stinging criticism you must level at employees, questions also save you from babbling. Many new managers tend to express criticism by talking so much that they leave their employee feeling like a scolded preschooler. Strive to establish a speak-listen rhythm so that you don't wind up repeating yourself and using language that's unduly harsh.

Questions also help you avoid lapsing into a lecturing mode. The more you discuss how "unhappy" you are or how vital it is that "screw-ups not occur on my watch," the more you'll shake your employee's confidence and willingness to improve. You may feel you've gotten something off your chest, but the other person will walk away like a wounded animal or simply assume you're an overly critical adversary rather than a decent boss.

What's worse, if you talk too much, you risk coming across like an amateur psychologist. You may start dishing out diagnoses that attempt to explain why an employee isn't performing better, ranging from "a negative, destructive attitude" to "a stubborn insistence to do things your way." The more you talk, the more likely you will say something that will antagonize your staffers and kill any hopes of giving well-received criticism.

Connect Past to Future

New managers often think criticism consists of explaining something that someone did wrong. That's only partially right.

In fact, there's another stage to effective criticism: showing your employee how to improve in the future. You need to mix your analysis of past actions with a forward-looking prescription for how the individual can perform better. For instance, telling your aide that he didn't do a good job setting priorities doesn't help him organize his time better. You need to tie the fact that he didn't set priorities well with steps he can take from now on to accomplish more pressing tasks in a systematic way.

Simply instructing your employee to do better won't suffice. "You've got to shape up" comes across more as a vague threat than a rallying cry that will raise the worker's spirits. Instead, prod the individual to draft an action plan that gives a step-by-step process for fixing what's broken. Have your employee write down possible solution steps and work together to finalize an approach that both of you think will lead to the necessary improvement.

By directing the employee to think in terms of positive change, you turn a potentially devastating, morale-harming attack into constructive criticism. Labeling someone's work as "bad—leaves a lot to be desired" is like the kiss of death. But if you say, "That work left a lot to be desired. In the future, develop your ideas more fully with examples, projections, and at

---

YOU PICK THE SOLUTION — SMART MANAGING

Before you criticize someone for poor performance, identify at least three specific steps that individual can take to improve. These can include adopting better project management skills, working with a mentor, or completing an online self-study course to plug learning gaps. That way, you can follow up your criticism of past actions by saying, "Now it's up to you to learn from this and improve. Here are some possible ways to do that."

Solution steps — KEY TERM

The specific actions and behaviors an employee commits to doing in order to address your criticism and enhance performance. While you can suggest possible steps, it's the employee's responsibility to define them and decide which ones to implement.

least some consideration of the downside," you provide a road map for professional growth.

The danger of dwelling on past failings without tying them to future improvements is that you can leave your employees feeling angry and unsure of their ability. They may avoid you, figuring that keeping a low profile will lower the odds that you'll cut them down. And they may try to avoid resuming the work that you criticized, fearing that they just can't get it right. You need to leave the employee with a sense of hope that the next time will be better, and that the two of you have agreed on solution steps that make sense.

Avoid Criticism That Bites Back

We've already warned you that it's dangerous to attack someone's personality when you criticize. Stick to specific behavior and you'll have a positive impact.

But that's not the only pitfall of dishing out criticism. New managers face many other traps when they decide to make an employee aware that there's a performance-related problem he or she needs to improve. Here are five examples of mistakes to avoid:

Applying the "sandwich" technique. Some schoolteachers are taught to give children criticism by mixing good comments with bad ones. Youngsters are more open to negative feedback if it's blended with compliments, according to conventional wisdom. While that may prove true for seven-year-olds, it's not necessarily a smart way to handle your employees. If you sandwich something bad between two slices of praise, most workers will see through your ploy and dwell solely on the criticism. Your positive remarks will sound forced, like you were applying a technique. Example: "You're very bright, Alex, but you're too arrogant. You rub people the wrong way, and you tend to alienate your teammates. I know you're conscientious, and that's something I admire about you." It's a safe bet that Alex will walk away thinking "I'm arrogant?" or "I rub people the wrong way?" and "I alienate my teammates?" rather than "It's nice to know my boss thinks I'm bright and conscientious." Always look for opportunities to praise, but make it genuine. Don't detract from it by tossing in criticism that drowns out the praise.

Letting the blind lead the blind. Never criticize what you don't understand. New managers may assume it's their job to point out employees' flaws and correct them, even if they don't really know what they're talking about. This often happens when a technician gets promoted into a position of people management. The newly installed manager notices an employee who's struggling to design a financial spreadsheet, so he criticizes the worker for "doing it wrong" and then says, "Here, let me show you how to do it right." After a few minutes of fruitless experimentation, the manager realizes he has no idea what he's doing. He's winging it. Had the manager refrained from criticizing and instead tried to fiddle with the program alongside the employee so that they could learn together, they could have bonded a bit without undermining the subordinate's confidence.

> ## My Mistake, Not Yours
>
> Adults, like children, rarely enjoy acknowledging their own blunders. But they find it easy and often satisfying to point out other people's mistakes. Keep this in mind when weighing how and whether to criticize an employee. Before you give feedback—even well-intentioned, politely worded feedback—ask yourself, "Have I admitted my own mistakes as they relate to this issue?"

Hogging the spotlight. If you get nervous when you're about to criticize someone, you may alleviate your jitters by talking about a subject you're much more comfortable with: you. Rather than describe your concern clearly and propose a solution that helps your employee perform better, you may lapse into a monologue in which you discuss your own upset, worries, or experiences that may or may not relate to the issue at hand. In a role-play during one of my management training seminars, I asked a new manager to practice criticizing an employee. But he didn't talk about the other person's work product; instead, he spent five minutes repeating how "let down" and "dismayed" he felt in dealing with his employee. Finally I said, "You've made it clear how *you* feel. Now give your employee some helpful criticism, or you'll risk dominating the conversation."

Making a spectacle. Never criticize an employee in front of others. Remember that you want to leave the individual feeling confident and motivated to improve. If you express your concerns in public, you can embarrass and even humiliate the person you're trying to help. Some managers mistakenly think it's fine to criticize someone with others watching—that teaching a lesson in front of onlookers increases the odds it will sink in. You're playing with fire. Criticism is hard enough for most of us to take in private when communicated in a supportive manner. But when it's delivered in a crowded staff meeting, you're almost guaranteed you'll create tension. Even seemingly harmless comments such as "That's not how we do things around here" or "You're not trying very hard, are you?" can prove hurtful and send a message that you're more of a harsh judge than a judicious manager.

Rushing to advise. There's a subtle difference between giving advice and making a suggestion. Advice involves telling someone how to solve a problem. It can include specific steps, actions, or instructions. Suggestions do not tell people what to do as much as offer hints, insights, or observations. The listener can choose to embrace or reject suggestions, which are softer and less direct than straight advice. When you're criticizing employees, don't hop right to the advice-giving stage. First pinpoint the action that you observed and describe it fully and accurately. Then show your interest in the worker's point of view, asking questions and maintaining a balanced speak-listen ratio so that you both contribute to the conversation. Ideally, you want your employee to ask, "Say, do you have any ideas on how I can improve?" That gives you an opening to advise. But in most cases, it won't prove so easy to bark out do-this, do-that commands. That's why you should lay off the advice and stick to safe suggestions that enable employees to think for themselves and draw their own conclusions.

Even if you steer clear of all of the traps listed above, you still need to pay attention to your tone and body language. Don't raise your voice or sound upset when you criticize. Speak in your normal, conversational style. In fact, it's fine to radiate a dose of enthusiasm when you criticize. That's right—you don't need to dread what you say and wear your "this is dead serious" face. As long as your comments are sincere and blame free, there's no reason to sound hesitant, stern, or downbeat.

Don't frown, grimace, or otherwise appear gloomy or annoyed. If you're nervous inside, you may unleash your anxiety by speaking in a

> ### USE "ICE" WHEN YOU CRITICIZE
>
> **TRICKS OF THE TRADE**
>
> Here's an easy, three-step process to help you criticize better. Begin by greeting your employee and making an "I" statement, such as "I have a problem" or "I'm concerned about something, and it involves your performance." Then contrast the type of action you need with what the employee's doing. Example: "I need to know the numbers on the weekly activity report are completely accurate, but for the past month I've found several errors." Third, ask for an explanation in a nonthreatening tone, such as "Could you help me understand what's going on?" or "Explain to me what's happening." Through the ICE approach (I statements–Contrast behavior–Explain), you can work with the employee to hash out a solution.

more tense or agitated manner. Control your fear so that your nervousness does not envelop the room.

The safest and smartest criticism comes across as a gentle form of supportive, well-intentioned awareness raising, not as a red flag frantically waving in front of an employee's panicked and bewildered face. You want to share observations and seek information to help your employee succeed, not assert your superiority by proclaiming, "I told you that wouldn't work" or "You're just too impatient and aggressive." Like a friendly but curious detective (think TV's Lieutenant Colombo), you want to investigate behavior rather than take sides and assign right-wrong labels prematurely.

New Manager's Checklist for Chapter 7

☑ Focus your criticism on an employee's specific behaviors or actions, not on personality.

☑ Report "just the facts" by saying what you see. Don't assign blame or label the behavior.

☑ Avoid using the words *always, never,* and *worst.* And don't follow *you* with a negative such as "You didn't ..." or "You won't ...."

☑ Ask questions when you criticize to encourage your employees to do your work for you. Prod them to evaluate their performance honestly in a nonthreatening atmosphere.

☑ Provide forward-looking criticism that ties past actions to future improvements.

☑ Never criticize what you do not understand.

Speak in a supportive, conversational tone when you criticize. Don't raise your voice or sound upset.

Discipline That Pays Off

When Dave learned that his employee lied about some lost invoices, he knew he had to figure out a fair but tough way to address such misbehavior. But he had no idea what to do.

Should he berate the individual and demand an apology? Or should he go a step further and write up the incident to add to the personnel file? Then there was the harsh step of employment probation—a more formal and high-stakes way to send a message that Dave would not tolerate lying.

Most new managers have no blueprint to follow when doling out discipline. It's almost always a judgment call, and that makes it a hornet's nest in more ways than one. If you're too soft, you risk inviting more of the same kind of unacceptable actions. If you're too hard-nosed, you can gain a reputation as an inflexible tyrant who goes overboard and has no sense of perspective. And if you ignore it entirely or postpone a decision on how to respond, you undermine the whole process by waiting too long.

What's at Stake?

The biggest mistake rookie managers make when having to discipline their staff is they react impulsively. Rather than planning what they want to say and do based on an objective analysis of the facts, they lash out and let their emotions interfere. Instead of isolating the specific wrongdoing and determining why it matters, they rush to put their foot down because they feel an employee has betrayed their trust, a costly miscue will slow the unit's progress, or they're simply fed up and need to unleash their frustration.

To avoid falling into this trap, make sure you know what's at stake before you exert discipline. Ask yourself three sets of questions:

1. **Repercussions.** What short- and long-term harm can this behavior cause? Could the employee have foreseen such harm?

2. **Rationale.** Are there mitigating factors? For example, did the individual have at least some positive reasons or valid motives for acting up? Was the employee under the impression there was a greater good to be gained that outweighed the wrongdoing?

3. **Lessons.** What messages do you want to send through your choice of discipline? Do other employees and/or bosses care about this situation? Do they clearly know to what extent and why the employee's actions were wrong, or do you need to explain?

Many new managers lack an institutional history. They don't realize that other managers before them have probably dealt with the same or similar disciplinary challenges, and that precedent can provide helpful clues on how to respond. By investigating how such problems have been handled before, you can apply consistent punishment that aligns with your organizational culture.

 KEY TERM   **Precedent chain** A sequence of disciplinary measures that you and/or your predecessors have taken for the same type of offense. By linking to the chain of events that have come before, you can use precedent to guide your decision on applying the appropriate level of discipline.

Never view a single incident in isolation, detached from other types of problems. You can discipline an employee for hundreds of reasons, but they're almost all related in some way to what's come before. If possible, interview the outgoing manager to discuss how such matters were handled. Also check with a representative from human resources and—for serious incidents—an employment lawyer. Dig to determine how the past should influence the present course of action.

Disciplining the Uncooperative Pest

Lucky Stan. During his first month as a new supervisor, he didn't have to discipline any of his employees.

Yet one customer service rep soon became increasingly surly and unresponsive. Eventually, he refused to follow orders. But rather than say no, he simply laughed at Stan's requests and said, "Yeah, you better get out your whip and use that wet noodle to get me into shape."

Stan tried to reason with this person to no avail. Then he issued a few verbal warnings that bordered on threats, but his words seemed to fall on deaf ears (i.e., "If you don't shape up, I'm going to ..."). He began to feel as if his authority was on the line. That's when I was brought in to advise him.

Stan's first priority was to avoid threats he didn't intend to back up and instead communicate with steely determination and undeniable firmness. I told Stan he needed to speak in a concise, confident, and direct tone. That meant choosing his words more carefully and saying less but making them count more.

The best disciplinarians don't babble or repeat themselves in desperation; instead, they muzzle a malcontent with a stern look and a succinct warning that they utter slowly such as "Stop right there" or "Hold on now." They emphasize each word so that the message sinks in.

In Stan's case, the next time his employee attempted to reject or laugh off an instruction, Stan needed to put an end to such behavior. While listening often makes sense, a manager cannot remain passive when a subordinate continues to make inflammatory or insulting remarks.

"Make it clear you're serious and that you won't tolerate any more of this. Explain what needs to happen and what the consequences will be if it doesn't happen," I told Stan.

We practiced nonverbal cues that would help shut down inappropriate behavior, such as putting a hand up with his palm facing the employee as a signal to stop talking. We also examined the precedent chain at his company to decide what punishments would unfold if the behavior didn't improve, ranging from written warnings to probation to termination. Finally, we alerted Stan's boss of the situation so that everyone agreed on the best way to proceed. (New managers shouldn't hesitate to inform their

DON'T TAKE THE BAIT

Don't let your dislike of certain employees interfere with the way you discipline them. New managers can let difficult employees pull their strings and goad them into exploding or otherwise saying things they regret later. If you're angry or extremely irritable, detach yourself and regain your composure before you discuss disciplinary steps.

boss of a disciplinary problem to enlist the necessary support to clamp down on the undesirable behavior.)

How to Play Referee

If you supervise one individual, then you only have to worry about disciplining that person. But if you manage more than one employee, you may face off against two troublemakers who both get themselves in a mess. In those situations, you become a mediator as well as a manager. You must play the role of the unbiased, dispassionate referee.

Before you can mete out punishment, you need to investigate what happened and help bickering workers understand each other's position. That's a tall order, especially when tensions run high and rivals vie for your support. In these situations, discipline goes hand in hand with addressing misunderstandings and improving trust among your team.

SMART

MANAGING

ONE AT A TIME

When you need to discipline more than one employee, it's usually best to do so in private. Hold one-on-one discussions with each wrongdoer and emphasize how their performance must improve. Keep each conversation confidential. Disciplining employees should rarely be a public affair, because you want each individual to feel the full force of your actions—not bond with other employees who are in the same boat. And you never want to humiliate someone in front of coworkers.

Following a fair, systematic approach can ensure that you do not talk yourself into trouble and overstep your bounds. Here's a six-step process to help you discipline warring employees without having to bark orders like a tyrant.

1. **Get "I" statements.** Gather both employees in a room and ask each of them to state the problem. Have them start with "I" statements such as "I did" or "As I see it ...." Examples include "I did everything I

could to warn Wally about this, but he didn't listen to me" or "I felt I had no choice but to cut corners because Gene was making us fall behind schedule."

2. **Trade sides.** Now ask each employee to state the problem from the other's point of view. They should start by saying, "The way [their coworker's name] sees it . . . . " It may take a few tries before each person can step into the other person's shoes and explain the situation in a satisfactory manner. Have each participant confirm the accuracy of the other's restatement before you move to the next stage.

3. **Reinforce mutual needs.** Get both employees to nod and think, "Yes, that's important." Establish a base of agreement, a bedrock of understanding that both parties cannot help but acknowledge. "You both need to find a way to work together" or "All our jobs are at risk in this merger" can unify competitors and refocus everyone's attention on mutual goals.

4. **Collaborate on a solution.** Ask each worker to propose positive, productive steps to help everyone attain the mutual goals you've identified. If they're hesitant or simply don't have any sensible ideas, give them a day or two to ponder the problem and reconvene. Make it clear you expect both employees to propose specific recommendations, and that they will need to work together to implement a solution that all of you create.

5. **Dole out discipline.** Now's the time to penalize people or at least lay out the consequences of the employees' actions. First, arrange to see each employee privately. You might want to break for lunch and then allot ten minutes for a closed-door meeting with each participant. Use phrases such as "In view of your efforts today to work together, I'm going to be lenient" or "Normally, I'd dock your pay, but given your fine input and your willingness to learn from this, I'll go easy on you." This way, you still exert discipline—but it comes across as a somewhat gentle, positive outgrowth of your employees' collaboration rather than a stinging rebuke that breeds resentment.

6. **Set a timetable.** Conclude by mapping out the implementation of your employees' problem-solving scheme. Set preliminary and final deadlines to produce results. If you're punishing them, apply a time-

frame to this as well so that they'll know when they've finished paying for their misbehavior.

PUT IT IN WRITING

For the first step of asking employees to give "I" statements, you may want to have them write down their remarks. Many workers will describe their misbehavior more accurately on paper than if they talk about it. That's because they can inject ambiguities into their speech that they couldn't get away with or would be more reluctant to express in print. Plus, if a conflict arises about the facts, at least you'll have written summaries to compare each individual's version of events.

When you're disciplining an employee, keep the focus on that individual's performance. Don't let the worker shift the discussion to another person or try to pin blame on someone else. If you've already gathered the facts and confirmed them with all the parties, then there's no reason to rehash these issues. Tell the employee, "We're not here to talk about others. We're here to discuss *your* role and agree on the consequences of *your* actions."

Finally, don't expect everyone to accept your punishment with grace and good cheer. Discipline is an art, not a science. There's no single right answer in deciding how to respond to misbehavior. Sometimes you'll wind up being too soft; in other instances, you'll overreact and kick yourself later for blowing a relatively minor error out of proportion. And even if you're scrupulously fair in choosing how to discipline, your employees may not see it that way.

Don't fret if you feel like you've misfired in weighing how hard to put your foot down. Evaluate to what extent your disciplinary actions produce the desired long-term effect in your employees. It's a sad but true fact of management that you'll have plenty of other chances to practice how you exert discipline.

When to "Write Up" an Employee

Ruth learned that one of her employees said to a coworker, "That Ruth is really screwing us. She's a liar. Let's teach her a lesson and go over her head."

Like most bosses, you would probably be hurt and angry if you heard about such a vicious comment. But Ruth didn't sit and stew. Instead, she wrote up her employee for insubordination.

"The formality of putting a memo in this employee's personnel file struck me as appropriate under the circumstances," Ruth told me. "I wanted to send a message that you don't talk that way about your boss and get away with it. I want my people to know if they're going to be nasty and badmouth me or any other manager, then their behavior will be officially documented."

Fair enough. But rather than rush to write up an employee as Ruth did, it's often wise to treat this form of written discipline more carefully. After all, whenever you scold someone in writing, you magnify the incident by memorializing it in that individual's personnel record. It becomes a permanent piece of history, a black mark that can taint the employee's name over the long haul. While it underscores the seriousness of someone's behavior, it comes at a cost. You sow the seeds of mutual distrust and leave a trail of lasting ill will.

Here are three tests to help you weigh whether it's wise to discipline employees in writing:

1. Did you already hold a face-to-face meeting? Ruth was so furious that she didn't bother to contact the employee and ask, "Do you have a beef with me?" She assumed that what she heard through the grapevine was true, and she acted accordingly.

Never discipline others as an emotional reaction to upsetting news. It's a safe bet you'll either overdo it and exaggerate the importance of what happened or lose sight of the work-related issue and take the whole incident personally. New managers are especially susceptible to this dangerous rush to judgment, because they're new to the discipline game.

You must meet with the employee at some point, so you might as well talk it over and hear the employee's version of events *before* rather than after you write him or her up. Through a forthright, coolheaded dialogue, you can learn information that will provide a more complete understanding of the employee's motives and intentions. This in turn can help you figure out how to proceed.

2. Do you know the full story? Disciplining an employee is hard enough without having to separate fact from fiction. In many disputes, ambiguities make it hard for a manager to assign blame with any accuracy. If everyone agrees on the events in question—and those events clearly violated your company's policies—then you're on safe ground writing a disciplinary memo. And if you have evidence to prove what happened, such as a video camera that shows a theft in progress, then that's even better.

In many cases, confirming the facts is an exercise in futility. No matter how diligently you try to get to the bottom of a conflict or seek to explain an otherwise competent employee's lapse in judgment, you may never know what really happened or whom to believe.

DISCIPLINE WITHOUT RISK

CAUTION Don't make a decision about writing up an employee until you're certain about what happened. Your credibility is on the line, so make sure you're right. Cross-check every relevant fact with the parties involved so that you're sure you have correct information. If that's impossible, but you still feel compelled to take some kind of strong action, sit down with a presumably guilty individual and talk it out. Note whether the employee seems tense or defensive; making someone squirm can prove its own kind of tough discipline. Rather than try to know the unknowable, explain the levels of punishment that any worker can expect for certain types of wrongdoing.

3. Is the employee a repeat offender? Say you've already tried gentler forms of discipline, such as issuing oral warnings and denying the individual minor privileges. But the employee continues to perform unacceptably and shows no sign of trying to improve. Here's when it's wise to assert your authority.

A bluntly worded memo can drill home your displeasure with an employee's actions. Using statements such as "This behavior is unacceptable and will not be tolerated in the future" or "This puts you on notice that any further violation of company policy will result in further disciplinary action" can send a chill down an employee's spine.

Once you write such a memo, wait a day before you send it. Reread it to ensure you stick to the core issue and that you clearly explain what the employee did wrong, why it's wrong, and what will happen if such behavior continues.

Delete any inflammatory language or editorial asides that detract from your main message. For example, don't write, "I suspected that you would not heed my last warning" or "Your actions reveal an immaturity that has hurt your reputation in this organization." Such comments threaten to open a Pandora's box that's best left sealed. What's worse, an employee will probably dwell on these sentences and disregard the rest.

Getting Personal

You might as well learn this lesson now rather than later: it's unwise to turn a disciplinary message into a personal attack against the employee. That's one of those basic truths that most managers know, but few follow.

Rookie managers may think they're focusing on faulty, substandard performance when they discipline. But then they inject all kinds of inappropriate or overblown remarks that trigger antagonism. This applies to discipline expressed both in print and in person. Here are some examples of how *not* to launch a disciplinary discussion:

I'm at my wit's end with you. This keeps happening, and I'm ready to scream.

Your error rate is out of control. You don't seem to be making enough of an effort.

I give up trying to figure out your problem. It's beyond me.

In all my years of work, I've never faced anyone quite like you.

It seems apparent to me you don't treat our performance standards seriously.

Don't laugh. Maybe you wouldn't talk this way, but many otherwise tactful, well-intentioned managers do. And they aren't necessarily speaking in an insulting or malicious tone. In fact, they may be so nervous or uncomfortable with the prospect of having to discipline someone that they say things they regret later.

Aside from the fact that these types of opening salvos instantly turn an employee against you, your words signal that you're not in the mood for a fair, balanced dialogue. Instead, they may lead your employee to conclude that you're going to lecture, scold, and pontificate. Such a one-sided conversation is hardly conducive to changing someone's behavior in a positive way.

TOO MUCH "I"

FOR EXAMPLE
In her first few months as a manager, Fran could tell Barry's work was slipping. She warned him casually a few times, but now she opted for more formal discipline. First she rehearsed what she wanted to say to Barry: "You're letting me down. I used to work alongside you, so I've seen you at your best. Now whenever I come into your office, you act as if you're hiding something. It's like you'd rather play games than work. What's up?" I warned Fran that this approach wouldn't succeed because it was more about her perception and personal interpretations than the actual areas where Barry failed to meet performance standards.

Don't take potshots when you discipline. Avoid making innuendoes and analyzing *why* an employee has not produced quality work or has not followed the rules. The "why" isn't as important as clearly explaining what the person did and how that action or behavior fell below an acceptable standard.

New managers often wonder how to start a conversation when they know they must call someone on the carpet for poor work. The best strategy is to set a friendly, inquisitive tone and establish from the outset that you expect a give-and-take discussion. You might start off with an open-ended question, such as "Sue, you've been here two years now, and I'm curious whether you feel as if you're making progress in your job in finding effective ways to meet our performance standards. How do you think you're doing?"

It's often smart to begin by mentioning how long the individual has been employed at your organization. That instantly provides perspective and shows that you've done some research. It also can put the employee in a reflective or confessional mood. You may hear revealing responses such as a cheerful "Has it been that long!" or a doleful "Yeah, I have been here a long, long time."

Another benefit of opening the meeting in this manner is that you avoid volunteering your feelings or opinions too soon. You don't want to pounce on the employee from the start by expressing your disappointment or dismay at all that he has done wrong. This will inject a needlessly personal, adversarial tone into the discussion.

In addition to citing the employee's years of service at your organization, ask about his awareness of performance expectations. Use questions such as "Are you familiar with the performance standards that apply to your job?" or "In your last performance review with your previous supervisor, did you come away with a clear understanding of the minimum expectations for your role?"

Disciplinary meetings offer a good opportunity to clarify what you expect and how you measure performance. Review the metrics and organizational policies that you're using to evaluate the employee. That way, there's transparency when it comes to assessing performance and defining expectations.

DOING YOUR HOMEWORK

Before you discipline someone in person, invest a few minutes to read the employee's personnel file. Prepare a cheat sheet that you can refer to during the meeting. It should provide key facts at a glance, such as years/months of employment, past disciplinary problems, past accomplishments, and perhaps a list of previous positions, job titles, and bosses. This fact-finding will boost your confidence and demonstrate that you've taken an interest in the individual—rather than impulsively deciding to dish out punishment.

TOOLS

Beware of getting personal when an employee's attitude rubs you the wrong way. A scowling, sarcastic, or bitter individual can bring out the worst in you, so it's crucial to stick to the issue at hand and not react to negative personality traits. Realize that most people don't like to confront their substandard performance; they'd rather pretend as if everything's fine or at least avoid hearing their boss analyze how they're failing. Employees might respond with denial and rebellion—not forthright, chagrined acceptance.

If you try to describe how the employee's performance falls below what's acceptable—and you're greeted with derision or outright disagreement—resist the urge to contradict ("No, you're wrong!") or make a personal attack ("Where do you come off saying that to me?"). Instead, remain dispassionate and say in a nonthreatening tone, "We see things differently. Based on my observation and these activity reports, it's clear your performance doesn't meet the standards we've set for the job. Can you figure out why we're apart on this?"

This approach invites a more searching, honest dialogue. Employees

MILD, MEDIUM, AND HOT
To avoid inflammatory remarks that only provoke a personal feud, begin your discussion in a positive, unfettered frame of mind. Banish thoughts of dread such as "I hate doing this." Instead, describe in unambiguous terms what qualifies as satisfactory behavior and how the employee's actions have not met this threshold. If the employee bristles or fights back, imagine that you can choose between a mild, medium, and hot reply. Start with mild. Don't give yourself permission to escalate the battle by displaying a medium or hot reaction. This reminder can save you from losing your temper.

will appreciate the chance to state their case, even if you privately suspect it's built on excuses. By listening patiently, you gain credibility and solidify your position as a sensitive, fair-minded boss who doesn't rush to discipline without hearing all sides.

Discipline That Sticks

If you're going to discipline, you might as well make it count. Saying, "I'm unhappy with your work" or "I leave it up to you to find a way to improve" won't suffice. Such vague comments rarely lift an individual's performance on their own. You need to provide more direct, specific guidance.

If you know that a staffer's behavior is unacceptable and merits punishment of some sort—but you're unsure what's appropriate—then lay out three possible disciplinary steps you can take and let the employee decide which one applies. For example, you can say, "Given what you've done, I can either demote you so that you no longer interact with customers, require that you design and lead a training program to help others avoid this mistake, or write you up and put you on probation. Which one would you choose?"

By allowing the employee to select the specific punishment, you achieve three goals. First, you increase the odds the individual will rebound from the misbehavior and perform more effectively in the future. The worker becomes a participant in the disciplinary process, not a spectator awaiting bad news. Second, you avoid having to decide what course of action to take. New managers may lack experience doling out discipline, so by providing a menu of choices, you let yourself off the hook to some degree. Finally, you can learn more about how an employee thinks by noting which punishment is chosen. It's another way to get to know what makes your staffers tick.

Another approach to put teeth into your discipline is to help the employee trace a clear deterioration in performance. You may want to draw a timeline or graph that displays a steady decline in productivity, based on some objective measure such as orders processed per day or cases settled per day. Let the facts speak for themselves.

A final word about discipline: propose a way for the individual to show immediate improvement. Don't describe what went wrong and why that's unacceptable; insist that you see marked improvement by, say, next Friday—or you will take further action. Confirm that the employee understands the gravity of the situation and the need to produce better results or act more professionally *now*—not later.

New Manager's Checklist for Chapter 8

☑ Before you exert discipline, know the repercussions of the misbehavior, the rationale for what happened, and the lessons you want the employee to learn.

☑ Consider precedent when you discipline. Make sure you're being consistent when responding to similar types of wrongdoing.

☑ Discipline in private and focus on the actions, performance, or behavior that is unacceptable—not the employee's personality.

☑ Don't rush to write up an employee. Save this formal option for cases of serious wrongdoing when you've gathered facts and listened to all sides before making a judgment.

☑ Always read an employee's personnel file before you discipline.

☑ Give employees a choice of what they think is fair discipline from among three similar levels of punishment.

The Organized Manager

Todd's job kept him on the move. As a risk manager for a big corporation, he'd spend most days visiting field offices and inspecting their facilities for safety hazards. He didn't set a specific time for people to expect him at each stop, so he could make his own schedule and show up at branch offices whenever he wanted.

When Todd was promoted to supervisor, he needed to overhaul his approach to time management. He had meetings to attend, schedules to stick to, and activity reports to complete by set deadlines. Suddenly, the clock played a vital role in his daily job. He had to find a way to work more productively and sharpen his organizational skills.

Most new managers experience the same bracing realization. They're usually overwhelmed at first by the amount of work they face, and they question how they're supposed to get everything accomplished in an eight- or ten-hour day. Then they gradually find ways to work more efficiently or at least guard their time more carefully to eliminate waste.

For many managers, organizing doesn't come naturally. Don't let yourself off the hook that easily. "I'm not that efficient" or "Time management isn't my strong suit" are cop-out phrases. You're not born with organizational skills—you develop them. You need to find ways to get more done in less time, and that takes awareness and discipline.

If you want to hit the ground running as a new manager, take immediate steps to become more organized. The sooner you learn how to gain productivity, the faster you'll make an impact. Plus, your disciplined time management skills will set an example for others to follow. You will control the job—not vice versa.

Are You Running on Time?

The first step in sharpening your organizational skills is identifying your work habits. You must become more proactive about how you spend your time, rather than routinely letting events or people monopolize big chunks of your day.

Take this test to diagnose how well you manage your time and impose order on the chaos of everyday life.

Answer each of the following questions on a 1-to-10 scale, with 1 as "never," 5 as "half the time," and 10 as "always."

Meals. I skip breakfast or lunch because I'm in a rush or too busy to eat.

_____

Deadlines. I miss deadlines or do not complete assignments by the time I promised to. _____

Downtime. In between periods of doing real work, I'll go online for personal reasons. _____

Mishaps. When I've lost something like my eyeglasses or if my computer crashes, I'll drop everything and focus on the problem—-even if it takes an hour or two to fix. _____

Procrastination. When I dread a task or assignment, I'll repeatedly put it off. _____

Flexibility. When a sudden crisis needs my attention, I'll shift gears and address it only after I've taken care of other, relatively minor loose ends. _____

Awareness. I lose track of the time during the workday. _____

Clutter. I'm unable to work efficiently at my desk because of all the clutter.

_____

Meetings. I spend more time than necessary in meetings. _____

Scheduling. I overbook myself during the day, forcing me to run late habitually. _____

Total your score, which will range from 10 to 100. A result over 60 indicates a serious lack of organization. A score over 80 almost guarantees you won't last long in the management ranks because you're not operating efficiently. Most new managers score between 40 and 60, which means they can stand to improve but they're already somewhat organized. If your total falls below 40, then you're off to a great start.

Maximizing Each Hour

If your spouse complains that you're "so protective of your time," that's a red flag in a relationship. It's often better to go with the flow and not worry about squandering every precious moment.

But what works in your personal life may not translate to success in the office. That's because effective managers *must* protect their time. If they don't, they let circumstances control them and struggle to stick to a well-managed plan. Remaining flexible in the face of an emergency is wise, but showing too much willingness to jettison one task for another can leave you not accomplishing anything.

To boost your level of organization, know when you can produce the best results. Most managers can function at their absolute best during a certain hour of the day, whether it's early morning, just before lunch, or the late afternoon when most others have left and there's less noise and distractions. During this optimal hour, you can concentrate fully, finish what you start, and balance two or three tasks at once.

New managers often assume their optimal hour falls at the end of the day, when

Optimal hour The hour of the workday when you're able to perform most productively in your most focused, attentive, and inquisitive state. Smart managers reserve this period to tackle their most sensitive, demanding, or dreaded assignments.

KEY TERM

their employees have left and they can quietly regroup. But don't confuse your mop-up time when you rifle through paperwork with your peak work period when you can move beyond your daily chores.

To discover your optimal time, take 10 minutes next Sunday night to create a written schedule for the week ahead. Reserve a different one-hour chunk of time for each of the next five days. Example: Monday, 8:00–9:00 a.m.; Tuesday, 10:00–11:00 a.m.; Wednesday, 11:00 a.m.–12:00 p.m.; Thursday, 2:00–3:00 p.m.; Friday, 4:00–5:00 p.m.

Each day, set aside those designated hours for uninterrupted work. Don't take phone calls or see visitors during these times. After you com-

TRICKS OF THE TRADE

PROTECT YOUR PRIVATE TIME

Once you discover when you can function at your best, don't keep it a secret. Guard this hour religiously. Close your door, post a sign-up sheet to ward off interrupting visitors, and forward your incoming calls. Save your most challenging task for this hour and let everyone know that this time belongs to you.

plete each hour, evaluate your productivity. Assign a letter grade (A through F) based on how well you worked, how much you accomplished, and your energy level.

When the week's over, you can tell your optimal hour by analyzing which time received the highest grade. You may want to repeat this process for a second week and experiment with different hours, or block out the same hours again and evaluate whether you gave yourself the same grades for the same times.

Invest in the Future

Just as you put aside money in a retirement plan, you should take steps now to become more organized later. Savvy managers lay the groundwork so that when the inevitable crises erupt, those managers are well equipped to stay on track and remain productive. They don't get flustered because they've planned for the unexpected and cut themselves some slack to handle the rush of events.

Here are some strategies to anticipate time wasters and boost your standing as an unflappable, well-organized manager.

Make incremental progress. New managers often schedule their toughest or least liked activities, such as performance reviews or disciplinary meetings, without considering the time they'll need to prepare for such discussions. For example, they may line up a series of appraisals one after another on Monday morning, without factoring in the time they need to review each employee's personnel file and outline what they want to say.

Another mistake is to shrug off upcoming deadlines if there are still at least a few days left. But soon enough, the deadline day arrives, and the careless manager must play catch-up to get the work done.

A better approach is to organize your time so that you work steadily toward a goal. Commit to making at least some progress early and often, even if you're merely jotting some notes for a meeting that isn't scheduled for another week or two. And if you need to research an issue by talking to colleagues, initiate those calls now. That way you won't panic if you can't reach them right away or if they're out of the office for a few days.

Make a list for tomorrow, not today. Some managers don't bother to write a daily to-do list, which makes organization almost impossible. Others just scribble a few reminders when they arrive in the office every morning, which can induce stress as the phone starts ringing and fires break out. Within a few minutes of settling down to work, you can be overwhelmed and convinced you'll never find the time to refine your list, much less cross off anything!

The smartest, most efficient managers treat such lists more seriously. They write them the previous night so that they can wake up the next morning with the knowledge of what must get done that day. And by composing the list when they're calm and unhurried, they can think more clearly about what must get done and prioritize better.

Prepare to pause. Even the most disciplined managers cannot crank out excellent work for hours on end. Everyone needs a break, or at least a chance to activate different parts of the brain, throughout the day. That's why you should build in pockets of downtime when planning your day's activities. Budget your time

TIME-SAVING MOBILE APPS SMART MANAGING

When you take notes or write to-do lists, double your efficiency by using a mobile app. With Penultimate, iPhone and iPad users can jot notes and e-mail them instantly to employees. If you promise to send updated data to a client, for example, you can make a note to do so—and use your tablet PC to alert your assistant to start preparing the material immediately. There are an ever-growing number of low- and no-cost productivity apps for the Android operating system as well as iOS for Apple products.

STRIKE THE RIGHT BALANCE MISTAKE PROOFING

To improve your time management skills, don't force yourself to do too much in a limited period. Mental exhaustion will set in, and you'll produce inferior work. Instead, give yourself a mental break of about 10 minutes for every 90 minutes of sustained, high-powered work. This pause recharges your batteries so that you think more clearly.

generously so that you're more likely to work ahead of schedule rather than falling behind.

Pounce on promises. When you tell someone you'll do something, do it now. Don't procrastinate and assume you'll remember it later. New managers often find themselves telling employees, "I don't know, but I'll find out and get back to you." Write down every commitment you make, even if it's as simple as gathering some facts about the company's record retention policy or rules that govern the use of social media.

Another benefit of following up on requests is that you avoid making people nag you later. For example, if a colleague proposes a practical pointer on Monday, apply it right away and report back by Friday on what you learned thanks to the suggestion. If you don't initiate this type of progress report, you may be interrupted when the person calls you back to ask if you've acted on the advice yet.

You don't even need to talk to the colleague. To save time, e-mail the individual with an update while expressing thanks.

Banishing Time Wasters

Organized managers cannot operate on autopilot. They must fight off forces that sap their time and energy. If they're too complacent, then they'll wind up reacting to the rush of events rather than imposing some kind of steely discipline on their workday.

The most insidious time wasters are also the hardest to resist. Here's how to overcome three of the toughest threats to maintaining an efficient schedule: engaging in wasteful or annoying conversations, dreading tasks you don't like, and squandering pockets of downtime.

From "Harmless" Chats to Knock-Down Arguments

Valerie loves to talk. Her employees grumble that she's a compulsive blabbermouth, and they try to avoid her during the workday. When she corners you, she'll gab about topics unrelated to the job—and she'll toss in dozens of long-winded examples or anecdotes on topics far afield from anything you need (or want) to know.

Aside from the fact that Valerie's penchant for blabbing undermines her productivity as a manager, it also distances her from her staff. They are less likely to ask questions and share concerns because they know they'll get caught in a whirlwind of chatter.

While there's nothing wrong with building rapport with your employees and remaining accessible to them, you can waste as much as an hour a day if you fail to express your points succinctly and move on. The most organized managers stick to the topic at hand. By asking questions and making concise statements, they don't hog the spotlight. And they treat each encounter as a chance to learn something from an employee, not as a leisurely opportunity to shoot the breeze.

Are You an Organized Communicator?

SMART MANAGING

To test whether you communicate effectively without wasting your time and others' time, monitor how you respond to requests. The next time an employee asks you a question, make sure the first sentence out of your mouth answers it (examples: *yes, no, it depends*). Use the second sentence to elaborate on your answer, without adding lots of extraneous information. Finally, check whether you kept your entire answer to five sentences or less. That's a desirable goal, because it quickly enables the questioner to follow up or ask for clarification.

Another way to improve your organizational skills is to put unsatisfying or aggravating conversations in perspective. You'll sabotage your productivity if you dwell on an argument and rehash it 20 times in your head. Just because you traded barbs with a smart-mouthed employee doesn't mean you must let it bother you for the rest of the day.

Think of managing as a numbers game. On any given day, you may engage in 25 to 50 separate conversations with employees. Odds are at least one of those interactions will cause some problems or leave you angry. If you allow these isolated instances of bickering to haunt you or prevent you from focusing on other tasks, then you won't operate at peak efficiency. Remind yourself of all the dialogues that go well, not the few that lead to conflicts.

Conquer "Anticipatory Dread"

New managers must tackle a range of duties that they never had to worry about before. Examples include criticizing an employee's poor work, conducting performance reviews, giving presentations at management meetings, and processing mountains of paperwork.

If you're well organized, then you dive right in and get these tasks accomplished with machine-like efficiency. But many managers don't work that way, at least in their first year on the job. Instead, they devote lots of time to dreading their responsibilities or simply complaining about them to whoever will listen. For every 10 minutes of whining, they may invest 1 minute of actual work. That's a ratio sure to lead to trouble.

Anticipatory dread The tendency to think ahead to tasks or job responsibilities **KEY TERM** that you don't like and dwell on how much you dread such work. This forward-looking dread often combines elements of pessimism, cynicism, and fear, and it can lead you to distort the actual task and blow it out of proportion.

To avoid "anticipatory dread," you need to replace negative thoughts with encouragement or optimism. Don't keep telling yourself (and confessing to others) that you "hate having to do this" or "can't stand this part of my job." Each time you remind yourself how much you dislike something, you squander precious time and give yourself an excuse to procrastinate. What's worse, you reinforce how much you dread it by repeatedly acknowledging that dread.

A better approach is to take a more expansive view. Rather than magnify one unpleasant task that awaits you, remind yourself that "this will only take 30 minutes out of my 50-hour week" or "I'm lucky, because this could be a lot worse."

Capitalizing on Downtime

There's nothing wrong with taking a breather when you're in the midst of hard work. But if you find yourself without any pressing duties and it's a slow day, you may give yourself permission to kick back and enjoy it.

Don't get too comfy.

Organized managers never let themselves coast through the easy times. They welcome seasonal lulls in activity or even a 15-minute block of unscheduled time during an otherwise busy week as a chance to regroup, prepare for hectic times ahead, and consider big-picture affairs.

Use your next pocket of downtime to set up "start deadlines." These are specific times within which you must get started on an assignment. By listing those to-do projects that you need to address in the coming months and deciding when you must begin to make progress on each of them, you give yourself a road map to stay organized and systematic in your approach.

While you should also establish due dates when you must complete projects, start

> ### KILLING TIME
> Beware of gorging on the Internet at work. According to a 2012 survey by Salary.com, 64 percent of employees admit visiting nonwork websites daily. They're checking e-mail, browsing news and entertainment sites, tracking social media, shopping online, and even job-hunting via LinkedIn or other networking sites.
>
> **CAUTION**

deadlines play an equally important role. The sooner you get underway, the more time you allot to make progress free from undue pressure or last-minute snafus.

The lure of downtime, coupled with the Internet, is that you'll think, "I'm just going to go online and see where it takes me. I'm sure I'll wind up doing something worthwhile." Thirty minutes later, you've learned nothing and gained nothing except steering yourself into a web-based mental fog.

One of the smartest ways to capitalize on downtime is to initiate contact with employees whom you might otherwise ignore. For example, call employees who work offsite and ask how they're doing. Let them report on their current activities and the latest news from the front. Begin by telling them how much time you have to chat: "I have 10 minutes before I need to get to a meeting, so I wanted to catch up and find out how it's going."

> ### MAKING SENSE OF YOUR FILES
> Here's a way to organize your files and improve your record keeping: Choose relevant categories to archive e-mails and other reference materials you want to save. Avoid overly broad labels such as "Pending," "Background" or "Active." Such terms are too general to help you retrieve specific information. Instead, select more descriptive tags such as "Purchasing Contracts," "Marketing Reports," "Employee Benefits," and "Software Updates." You'll wind up with more files, but they'll each contain material that's targeted to your needs.
>
> **TOOLS**

Showcasing Your Organizational Skills

If you've applied every tool mentioned so far in this chapter and you're now the most organized manager at your organization, don't congratulate yourself yet. Operating at peak efficiency is not enough. You also need to create the unmistakable impression that you're well organized.

When your colleagues, bosses, and employees perceive you as a productive, can-do manager who follows through with dependability and doesn't squander a second, then they will place a higher value on your time. They will put more trust in your judgments and gain confidence in your ability to tackle many challenges at once.

To demonstrate that you possess superb organizational skills, make them easy for all to see. For example, keep your office clean and don't keep visitors waiting while you fiddle with your tablet PC to find something you want to show them. And if you need to run to a meeting, don't wait to the last minute to grab all the materials you must bring; instead, gather them ahead of time so that you can stroll out of your office while talking with someone—without having to assemble items in a frantic rush.

Here are five ways to ensure that others cannot help but notice and admire your excellent organizational skills:

1. **Give updates.** Deliver on your promises. If you say you're going to do something, either do it right away or keep the other person apprised of your progress. Never force people to nag you and ask, "So what's going on with that project you said you'd get done last week?"

2. **Put it in writing.** Always carry a notepad (electronic or old-fashioned) and jot to-do reminders or instructions that others give you. Taking notes on what people say shows that you treat what you hear seriously and you intend to follow through. Think how you feel when you dine at a restaurant and the server tries to memorize a long order without using a pad. You worry that you'll get the wrong dish or it won't be prepared as you requested. Same goes when coworkers give you lots of data and you don't take visible steps—such as taking notes—to retain it all.

3. **Confirm key facts.** When someone gives you specific information, repeat it to confirm accuracy and prove that you've heard and

understood it. Examples include the date and time of a meeting, the full name and contact information of someone you're supposed to look up on a business trip, and the timetable for a project. Organized managers like to nail down specifics rather than settle for ambiguity. They'll take out their tablets or day planners and enter appointments right away, reassuring the other person that they intend to follow through.

4. **Post your whereabouts.** Some managers plant themselves in their office and barely move the whole day. As a result, they're easily accessible. But if your job requires you to attend lots of meetings or circulate throughout the office or factory floor, then you may want to post each day's schedule online or on your office door to help others track you down. Encourage them to e-mail or call you if you're off-site.

5. **Keep your office tidy.** Don't glamorize sloppiness by allowing big piles to accumulate on your desk or the floor. Some professionals, such as lawyers, bank loan officers, and insurance underwriters, tend to let files stack up around their office. But when you become a manager, leaving pending work strewn around can lead others to think you're unable to handle the burdens of the job. They may view you as a disorganized mess, and that can influence how they respond to your authority. Avoid clutter, even if you know where everything's kept. Make a sweep of your office at least once a day to clear away debris, empty your inbox and file stray documents.

Making Meetings Work

You've probably attended plenty of meetings, but now that you're a manager your presence will take on a whole new meaning. You'll need to anticipate issues that might get raised and come prepared to answer tough questions. If you're disorganized, you'll lose credibility and the chance to win over others.

Beware of taking a laissez faire attitude at meetings. Don't sit back and let colleagues or staffers babble at will. Many teams get bogged down in needless, time-consuming blather because the group leader's poor organizational skills tend to drag down everyone. Set the proper tone by distributing a clear agenda, inviting the appropriate people (and no one

SMART MANAGING

A Precise Agenda

When writing an agenda for a meeting, adopt an organized approach. Set exact times for each segment. For example, block out 10:15–10:55 to assess customer surveys, rather than 10:00–11:00. Schedule another topic at 11:00 sharp. This way, if participants want to take a break, they'll need to end no later than 10:55 to earn those extra five minutes.

else!), and sticking to your schedule.

To direct a meeting efficiently, keep it moving forward. Clearly inform the group of what questions need addressing and what issues deserve attention. Write a key problem on a flip chart and emphasize that your goal is to leave the room with at least three specific solutions. If someone veers off on a tangent, gesture to the flip chart as a silent reminder to stick to the core issue. If the speaker continues to ramble, interrupt by reminding everyone of the time. Say, "Because we only have another 45 minutes, let me jump in and keep us focused on the topic at hand."

If you want to generate buy-in from your staff or show that you listen to their concerns, don't throw the meeting open to general discussion. You may lose control of the proceedings as participants raise concerns that stray too far from the more important priorities you need to cover.

A smarter strategy is to meet privately with influential staffers to let them vent their frustrations or propose their ideas. That way, you can avoid facing runaway meetings where strong-willed individuals attempt to hijack the agenda.

FOR EXAMPLE

Saving Staff Meetings

When Trish became marketing manager, she continued her predecessor's habit of holding Monday staff meetings. But within a few weeks, she concluded these meetings were time wasters. She tried to impose an agenda, but the group simply used the meetings to complain about various personnel matters. Trish decided to take three steps to improve the situation. First, she met with the most vocal whiners ahead of time so that they wouldn't monopolize the meeting. Second, she locked the door at exactly 7:50 a.m. so that latecomers couldn't disrupt the group. Finally, she arrived early and wrote three words on the flip chart that signified the three most critical topics she wanted to cover. This way, everyone could see where the meeting was heading and what mattered most.

The most effective managers turn meetings into short, productive sessions when decisions get made quickly and employees participate in a collective effort to solve problems. By applying a laser-like focus to these gatherings, you can manage your time wisely while modeling for your employees how to stay organized and fight off distractions.

New Manager's Checklist for Chapter 9

☑ Review whether your work habits help you save time or squander it.

☑ Identify the time of the day when you operate at peak productivity and guard that time so that you can capitalize on it.

☑ When facing big projects, start early and make incremental progress. Don't wait too long to dive in.

☑ Write to-do lists the night before, rather than once you've arrived at your desk in the morning.

☑ Avoid "anticipatory dread" by not dwelling on how much you don't like to perform certain tasks. Plow ahead without making it harder on yourself.

☑ Run speedy meetings. Distribute a clear agenda, watch the clock, and interrupt babblers to keep everyone on track.

Delegating the Right Way

I f one more supposed 'expert' tells me I need to do a better job delegating, I'll kill 'em."

I could tell by the way Walt looked at me when he said this that he had reached his breaking point. A supervisor of a seven-person back-office staff for the last two years, Walt routinely worked 11-hour days. His boss asked me to meet with Walt to make sure the hardworking supervisor didn't burn out.

As soon as I raised the issue of lightening his load, he shot back, "I've tried everything. There's only so much my employees can do. Believe me, it's not like I insist on doing everything. I'd love it if I could sit back and depend on them more."

The more I spoke with Walt, the clearer the problem became. He assumed he had to do the work himself for it to get done properly. His boss held him accountable for producing certain results, and the only way he knew he could deliver was to personally perform those tasks that his staff seemed reluctant, unqualified, or downright unwilling to do.

Without sounding too much like a stuffy consultant, I explained to Walt that his work habits perpetuated a no-win, downhill spiral. I helped him realize that his belief that he could do things better than his employees might make him feel good, but it ultimately undermined his ability to manage and advance his career.

An organizational psychologist might diagnose Walt as having a *self-enhancement bias*. He inflated his own sense of importance by repeatedly claiming that he had skills, talents, experience, and intuitive ability that far exceeded anyone on his staff. As a result, he sighed and said that he "had to do it all" or else his unit's work would suffer.

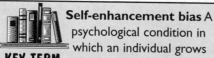

Self-enhancement bias A psychological condition in which an individual grows **KEY TERM** convinced that he's the only one who can produce the necessary level of acceptable work. To perpetuate this bias, the individual disregards or downplays employees' skills, attitudes, and contributions.

Evidence of self-enhancement bias surfaces every day in workplaces across the country. For example, most new managers readily admit that they're more qualified to do their employees' work than their employees are. A recently promoted technician will have more confidence in her own skills than in her employees' prowess. A new personnel manager will trust his instincts on whom to hire more than the judgments of other interviewers. An accounting manager will spend an extra 30 minutes reviewing her staff's number-crunching because "I trust my work 100 percent, but not theirs."

This explains why delegating poses such a challenge to so many supervisors, especially rookie managers who are used to doing the work themselves rather than having to oversee others' efforts. If you believe that there's a correlation between the amount of control you exert over a project and the quality of the results, then you'll micromanage everything.

Loosening Your Grip

As a new manager, you must accept one hard fact: you can't do it all.

Your success depends on the contributions of your employees. If they grow and continually sharpen their skills, then they'll not only become more valuable assets but will also perform their work with more enthusiasm, curiosity, and confidence.

Sounds great, doesn't it? All you have to do is lay off and let them make headway on their own. Resist the urge to step in to finish what they start. Realize that even though you need to wait another 10 minutes for someone to complete a task that you could've breezed through, those 10 minutes are a wise investment in the future. You'll save dozens of hours over the long run by giving employees enough time to grapple with tasks and gain the experience they need to improve.

Many supervisors understand the benefits of delegation, at least on an intellectual level. But they still hesitate to follow through and do it. The problem is often a lack of training. In a 2007 study by the Institute for Corporate Productivity, 46 percent of companies reported "somewhat high" or "high" level of concern about employees' delegation skills. But only 28 percent of the companies offered training to help managers delegate effectively.

If you find it hard to loosen your grip, consider the worst-case scenario if you delegate and things go awry. Errors can occur, but you can fix them. And there'll even be an upside: employees who make mistakes and learn from them become more valuable to you, because they now know what *not* to do. Their experience becomes the greatest teacher of all.

Another obstacle to delegating involves time. Some new managers prefer to perform the work themselves because it's quicker to do it than to explain to someone else how to do it. That's the rationalization I hear most often when new managers refuse to delegate. My favorite reply is, "So you've calculated how much time you'll save over the next six months? The next year?"

It *can* save time to do a job yourself rather than teach an employee. Once. But by the second, third, or fourth time you do it, you'll start to fall into a time trap. Say you insist on checking certain equipment every week, even though your crew is perfectly capable of learning how to conduct competent inspections. But you dread having to explain all the steps to the process, so you do it yourself.

DELEGATE IN STEPS *TRICKS OF THE TRADE*

Force yourself to release the reins a bit by reviewing your to-do list for the day and turning over one entire task to an employee. Examples include having a staffer make five customer check-in calls or represent you and take notes in an informational meeting. When you delegate, set a time for the two of you to review how it went. Now here's the tough part: forget about it until your follow-up meeting. Don't interfere by hovering over the employee's desk or finding excuses to drop by while the work's getting done.

You figure it'll take about one hour to give your employees an overview of what to look for during inspections. Then you estimate another two hours per week for the first four weeks, as you review their work and remind them how to do it right. Within a month's time, you can pull back and let them take over completely, because you'll be satisfied they know what they're doing. At that point, you'll gain about an hour a week by not having to do the inspections yourself.

Over the next year, you would thus free up about 48 hours of your time—the equivalent of six full workdays—by investing a total of 9 hours in the first month showing employees how to manage this task. By taking the long view, it becomes clear how much time you'll save by delegating.

TOOLS

ALWAYS-SOMETIMES-NEVER
List all your ongoing work duties, from discussing client projects with colleagues to designing prototypes to planning meeting agendas. Next to each item, pick which of the three statements best captures your role: I always must do this, I sometimes must do this, I never need to do this. Most tasks do not require that you "always" take charge, so delegate the "sometimes" and "never" jobs as much as possible.

Don't assume that as a manager you must take a hands-on interest in each and every assignment. It's more important to spread responsibility among your team and hold them accountable for exercising it.

"Your most important task as a leader is to teach people how to think and ask the right questions so that the world doesn't go to hell if you take a day off," said Jeffrey Pfeffer, author of many management books and Stanford University professor of organizational behavior, in an interview for the *Harvard Business Review's* blog (blogs.hbr.org).

Giving Good Directions

Once you realize the long-term benefits of delegating, the next step is to communicate what you need your employees to do in a clear, effective manner. The way that you delegate largely determines whether your employees respond well and catch on fast.

New managers may have little practice giving instructions. They may repeat themselves, talk down to workers, or assume too much when explaining what has to get done. Such pitfalls can turn delegating into a disaster.

Here are five of the most common mistakes that rookie managers make when trying to delegate:

1. They "rush and run." If you're going to state your directions clearly, then don't delegate as an afterthought as you're heading out the door. By speaking in a fast tempo and then scurrying away, you risk leaving your employees befuddled and uncertain how to proceed. Remember: Many workers need extra time to process instructions and gain confidence that they understand how to follow them. If you deny them the opportunity to absorb what you say and ask questions, then you increase the odds of a misfire when they take over. And if you use acronyms or technical lingo, they may not even understand your vocabulary, much less your directive. What's worse, they may feel slighted by your hurried attempt to bark orders as you leave the room for something more "important."

2. They improvise poorly. If you're not sure of what you want someone to do, don't think out loud while trying to give instructions. Address your uncertainties ahead of time so that when you delegate, you can spell out exactly what must get accomplished and the best way for the employee to do it. If you leave too much ambiguity, you force others to guess what you meant. That almost guarantees problems in execution.

3. They overexplain. A surefire way to make employees feel dumb is to treat them like preschoolers. Don't delegate with the assumption that they're too slow or stupid to understand simple directions. If you needlessly repeat obvious points or speak in a condescending tone, you can alienate your staff. They may spend more time resenting your communication style than listening to the content of your message.

> **REPEAT AFTER ME** **SMART**
>
> To improve your direction-giving skills, don't repeat your instructions as you give them. You may think you're reinforcing key points, but this will make your employees feel like children. Instead, state your directions once and then ask, "Why don't you go over that with me?" or "Will you walk me through how you're going to do this so that we're both assured that I explained this well?"
>
> **MANAGING**

4. They forget to ask for a demo. Experienced managers learn that some employees may not want to admit that they don't understand something. Instead of saying, "I didn't catch that" or "I'm not sure what you mean," they may nod and pretend everything's fine. Don't let that happen. When you delegate, ask employees to demonstrate what you want them to do. Give feedback, offer advice, and praise their progress so that they gain confidence in their skills.

5. They dwell on deadlines. You don't often have the luxury of saying, "Get this done at your leisure." In most cases, you must give the employee a date when the work must be completed. Yet if you focus too much on the endpoint, you may encourage the worker to procrastinate. After all, repeatedly insisting that "this project is due three months from today" can sound like an eternity to an employee who's barely able to keep pace with his daily duties. It's smarter to set a date by which the staffer must begin the work, so that there's no excuse for putting it off. For example, say, "This job's due on October 1. It's now August 5. Can you give me a timetable of when you'll start the research, synthesize the data, and finalize your recommendations?"

The key to giving good directions is investing the time to communicate effectively. I knew a manager who delegated tasks by jotting a few hurried to-do notes and taping them on an employee's computer monitor. The worker would arrive at his desk in the morning and immediately howl at the prospect of having to decipher these cryptic instructions. Because the manager was almost always in meetings or out of the office, the employee couldn't ask questions to clarify the notes.

Treat delegating as a chance to build rapport with your employees. Chat with them about what needs to get done, how they intend to do it, and why it's important. That may mean spending 10 minutes rather than 2 minutes assigning a task, but the extra effort up front will pay off.

Choosing with Care

Most new managers know it's wise to delegate. After overcoming their inclination to do the work themselves, they realize it's in everyone's interest for them to spread the work around among their team. But they often overlook an important aspect of delegating: choosing the right employee.

Every worker brings strengths and weaknesses to the job. A researcher may access online information quickly and efficiently, but lack the communication skills to explain it succinctly. An accountant may crunch numbers well, but fear standing up to a powerful executive who wants to cook the books. A salesperson may excel at identifying promising prospects, but lack the perseverance to follow through and contact them.

You must select the best individual for the assignment. The number one delegation trap for new managers is to assume that the job is so simple that anyone can do it. As a result, they pluck a random employee and say, "Here's what I need done. Get to it." That's a recipe for disaster.

> ### Don't Play Favorites
> You like and trust certain employees. Perhaps you used to work alongside a few of them and you know they're reliable, competent professionals. So when you decide to delegate, you instantly turn to them. Problem is, if you only ask your best workers to help, then you waste the energy and potential of the rest of your crew. You may never learn if they can deliver even better results. When you put an average worker to the test by delegating a critical assignment, you boost that individual's confidence.

When you delegate, weigh whether you want to discuss the best way for the employee to proceed or say, "Do this by Friday" and leave it at that. If you want to engage in a true dialogue and hear how the worker intends to follow through, then you want to choose someone who thinks independently and will speak up and share ideas openly with you. But for simple, straightforward tasks, you may not need to brainstorm or hash out a strategy for implementation.

After a few weeks as a manager, you can probably guess who among your staff will complain, resist, or challenge you when you ask them to do something. If you conclude that you're not going to bother delegating to these stubborn or strong-willed employees, then you'll wind up forcing the more obliging people to bear a heavier load. The result: they may eventually either turn into malcontents or burn out.

Mix and match whom you delegate to. Reserve time to "sell" at least some jobs to hardheaded or independent-minded employees. Prepare to debate with them the merits of different methods or approaches. Listen

TOOLS

RATE THE PLAYERS

To make sure you hand off assignments to everyone on your team, rate your employees on a 1-to-10 scale based on how they respond to delegation. Use 1 for the most quiet, pliant individuals; 10 for those who are the most stubborn or resistant. Then create a system so that for every easygoing employee with a rating of 5 or below to whom you delegate, you force yourself to assign projects to the more demanding staffers who rate 6 or higher. That way, you won't neglect to involve your more difficult employees—thus helping them develop their attitude and expand their skills.

with an open mind to their proposals to streamline the task. Welcome their input and praise them for suggesting sensible alternatives.

Ideally, you should delegate to employees who are motivated to follow through. Assign tasks to people who express interest in learning about those types of tasks.

As you get to know your employees, ask them what types of jobs they enjoy the most. Dig to discover their latent talents that you can tap. For example, a customer service representative who handles phone inquiries may yearn to visit customers face-to-face. She might make a good candidate to facilitate a focus group you're establishing or assist a sales associate on a client call. But unless you asked her, you would never know of her eagerness to interact with clients in person.

One way to learn about the kind of duties your employees like is to give each of them a sheet of paper and ask them to write their wish list of activities that they're interested in pursuing. They may list areas such as contributing to cross-departmental project teams, controlling a budget, or developing mobile apps.

Armed with this list, you can delegate certain jobs to workers who will pounce on them enthusiastically. This takes much of the guesswork out of determining who should do what among your staff.

When hiring employees, think ahead to how well they'll respond to delegation. Look for candidates who are highly intelligent doers with an entrepreneurial streak.

Sig Anderman, chief executive of Ellie Mae, which makes software for the residential mortgage industry, told me that he struggled with delegating early in his career. But he started recruiting job candidates who were smart problem solvers, and they turned into valuable employees who could handle any assignment he threw at them.

To assess intelligence, he'd ask candidates in interviews about their grades in college and even their SAT scores in high school. At age 70, Anderman has concluded after decades as a CEO that sharp thinkers who can figure out how to tackle any work-related task usually scored well on standardized tests back when they were students. In his view, individuals with a strong SAT score know how to apply reason, synthesize information under pressure, and make sound decisions.

Managing a Breakdown

The main reason managers dread delegating is that they fear the work won't get done. They can wind up having to scoop up the mess left by employees who either didn't understand or didn't remember to follow directions.

New managers must accept this harsh truth: some delegation will fail. Misunderstandings will occur. Managers, or their employees, will overlook details. Workers will lack the resources to follow through. Disruptions can make it impossible for them to deliver the work on time in a satisfactory manner.

But that's no reason to do everything yourself.

"I'd rather delegate work to someone else that gets done correctly 99 percent of the time, than have me do it right 100 percent of the time," says Jay Goltz, who owns five small businesses in Chicago and contributes to the "You're the Boss" blog for the *New York Times*. With more than 100 employees at his businesses to oversee, Goltz has learned to "manage his managers" so that he's free to run his operation without getting bogged down in minutiae.

By factoring in the few instances when your delegation will go awry, you can prepare yourself for those occasional breakdowns. Rather than use such sporadic disasters to justify micromanaging your staff, you should accept and learn from the occasional disaster.

When breakdowns occur, the cause usually revolves around sloppy communication or poor coordination. Either the manager doesn't explain

> ### DON'T DISAPPEAR AFTER YOU DELEGATE
> Once you assign a job to an employee, don't assume you can completely wash your hands of the situation. While you need not hover, you should remain accessible if the individual has questions along the way. If your employee seeks your guidance, for instance, it's better to give clear feedback (i.e., "Don't do it that way. Try this way instead.") rather than cast the worker adrift (i.e., "It's entirely your call.").

the task clearly, or the employee doesn't have the proper knowledge or tools to perform the task correctly.

The way you handle these mishaps will largely determine how your employees respond to your future attempts at delegation. If you explode in anger, they'll hesitate to try new approaches or take calculated risks to improve their results. They may also hide the facts from you and pretend everything's fine, only to let a bad situation get worse.

But if you react with equanimity, you assure employees that even the most costly blunders aren't going to rupture your relationship. Your calm, clearheaded response sends a message that you'd prefer to know the outcome right away—even if it's bad news.

Follow these guidelines when you learn your delegation has backfired:

Focus on solutions. Don't rush to assign blame in the midst of a snafu. After you gather the facts and confirm your understanding of what happened, dwelling on the problem only exacerbates it. Even if it appears obvious that your employee dropped the ball, don't judge too soon or express your disappointment too angrily. There will be time for assessments later and finger-pointing as you see fit. For now, maintain a forward-looking view. Prod your employee to weigh "what next?" questions. Work together to plot the best strategy to salvage the situation.

Keep your perspective. Some new managers aren't used to breakdowns. They may buckle under the pressure and blow their cool. You'll know that you've fallen into this trap if you start grumbling, "Why didn't I do this myself?" or "I knew I couldn't trust Bill to handle this." Contain your self-flagellation. Don't beat yourself mercilessly because your attempt at delegation failed. Remind yourself of the worst-case scenario and think of

---

Good Delegation, Bad Results

Razvan Olosu, CEO of a Germany-based tech firm called
Novero, told me that he has struggled with delegation for
much of his career. Before joining Novero in 2008, he was a
senior executive at Nokia where he oversaw 3,500 employees. At
Nokia, he'd delegate and sometimes hit minor bumps in the road. But at
Novero, botched delegation was more costly because with only 400
employees, every mistake was magnified. For instance, he asked an
employee to procure parts for products. When Olosu checked in a few
months later, he discovered soaring inventory costs because his employee
was buying six months of parts. Olosu assured him they didn't need to
acquire so many parts at once, and that conserving cash while pruning
inventory was more important.

---

the big picture. Chances are, this mess may annoy you now but will prove
to have little or no lasting impact.

Don't forget to dissect. Once you recover from the breakdown, wait a few
days and analyze it. Strive to learn from both your mistakes in how you
delegated the task and your employee's errors in following through.
Approach this not as a detective trying to find out who's guilty but as a
dispassionate reporter trying to assemble the facts accurately to shed
light on how events unfolded. Involve your employee in the process.
Politely explain that your goal is to extract lessons from the breakdown so
that it can be prevented in the future.

Bottom-Up Delegation

You may assume that delegation always travels downward, from the boss
to the subordinate. Actually, it works best when it arises out of a dialogue
between supervisor and staffer, where each person can contribute ideas
in order to finalize an action plan that the staffer will carry out.

Ideally, delegation should flow from discussions between managers
and staff where the boss describes a goal or challenge and invites workers to help define a solution. Most employees prefer to participate in a
joint search for knowledge rather than be spoon-fed exactly what they
need to know and what they must do as a result. If they're bossed around
every step of the way, they will turn into reactive zombies rather than
energetic, freethinking team members.

> **KEY TERM**
>
> **Participative delegation**
> The process of allowing your employees to partici-pate in crafting their own assignments and deciding the best way to implement them. This consists of dia-logues, such as brainstorming sessions and mutual problem solving, rather than one-way order giving.

To ensure that you apply participative delegation, get in the habit of asking your employees two questions: "Here's what I need done. How would you go about it?" and "What do you see as the pros and cons of that approach?" This trains them to consider the most efficient way to execute a plan, rather than blindly following your orders.

When employees play a role in shaping their assignment, they buy into it more forcefully. They'll also take ownership of the result.

Why? Because when workers know *why* they're doing something— and they help determine *how* they're going to get it done—then the odds of their success soar. They are fully engaged in the process, and this heightens their motivation and increases their level of concentration.

Here's how to prove it to yourself. Stage a two-prong experiment in which you first ask an employee to do something—with no questions asked and no discussion. Just give an order, make sure it's understood, and leave it at that. Then delegate the same task to another employee who shares a similar level of knowledge and experience. But this time, use participative delegation. Aside from the two questions above, you may want to ask, "What do you think about this?" and "What are your ideas on how to get this done?"

Compare the results. You'll probably find that the task is completed more effectively by the second employee. Better yet, this employee may provide a value-added bonus: rather than merely figuring out how to obtain your goal, he may propose additional ideas or uncover new ways to accomplish old tasks.

When you enable individuals to define the nature and scope of their work, they care about it more. And that not only leads to better results, but it makes your job as manager much easier.

New Manager's Checklist for Chapter 10

☑ You gain more control as a manager by giving it away in the form of delegation. Micromanaging creates built-in limitations.

☑ While you may save time in the short term by doing a job yourself, weigh the long-term costs of refusing to delegate.

☑ When giving directions, leave time to answer employees' questions and solicit their ideas.

☑ Supply key facts, such as the goal of the project and its deadline. But don't overexplain or provide too much information. This can make employees feel dumb.

☑ Don't play favorites when you delegate. Spread assignments around so that everyone's busy, while trying to match the type of work with individual strengths.

☑ If you delegate and the job doesn't get done properly, focus on solutions. Don't overreact or rush to pin blame on your employee.

New Manager's Checklist for Chapter 10

Managing
the Boss

Mark liked his boss. As a star computer programmer for a financial services firm, Mark felt that the best thing his boss could do was "stay out of my way." And Mark's boss happily complied.

But when Mark earned a promotion and became a manager, his boss could no longer leave him alone. Now the stakes were higher. Mark's responsibility didn't end with his own technical ability; his success as manager would depend on the accomplishments of others.

"When I became a manager, my boss suddenly took on a different role," Mark said. "Instead of trusting my judgment and letting me experiment, he would demand lots of information from me every week. He wanted to know what I was doing, what my employees were doing, what we planned to do the coming week, what problems we were having—it was like he had to know everything."

Mark confronted a common challenge that new managers face: how to satisfy their boss.

When you become a manager for the first time, it's natural for your boss to take an increased interest in your job performance. That's because you're moving from an area where you've proven yourself into uncharted terrain.

Upward Communication Traps

When you talk with your employees, there's always the chance for misunderstanding. You may give vague instructions, unclear explanations, or ambiguous answers to their questions.

When you talk with your boss, a whole new set of potential pitfalls can derail your communication. You may misinterpret an order as a suggestion, or vice versa. Or you may read meaning into a passing comment and assume the boss is trying to drop a subtle hint. Even the boss's jokes can cause anxiety if you think there's a message behind the humor.

When interacting with their boss, new managers often wonder, "What's he trying to tell me?" or "Am I missing something here?" Confusion can result, leaving the hapless manager playing a guessing game in trying to figure out exactly what the boss wants.

It's normal to feel a bit insecure at first. No one wants to look dumb and ask a boss, "What are you telling me?," "Can you speak more clearly?" or "Can you translate that into plain English?"

SMART

MANAGING

CLARIFY WITHOUT FEAR

Here's a tactic to cut through the boss's cryptic remarks and unearth the true message. Begin by saying, "Let me ask you a clarifying question." Then repeat something the boss said, verbatim. Close by asking, "Can you expand on that?" or "Is your intent then for me to …?" Some bosses will jump in the moment you repeat what they said, saving you from having to ask them anything. They may volunteer more information or explain their reasoning in more detail. In any case, it's important to parrot the words you heard—even if they make no sense to you. If you attempt to paraphrase, you invite more confusion.

Thus far we've discussed the danger of trying to decipher the boss's remarks. Let's not forget the traps that *you* can create by not speaking clearly. Problems can ensue if you're reluctant to level with your boss, provide specific information, or give bad news.

If your goal is to inform or educate your boss, avoid limiting yourself to general statements. Instead, lace your comments with facts such as dates, times, statistics, and performance metrics. The benefits are twofold: you show your boss how you've arrived at your conclusion, and you demonstrate your command of the kind of quantitative information that bosses can easily relay to *their* bosses.

If you want to win over your boss, then you also want to cite plenty of persuasive evidence to buttress your position. Ideally, you should succinctly summarize what you want your boss to do. Then think in threes (see Chapter 5) so that you give a trio of cogent, hard-hitting reasons why your boss should approve your proposal.

Regardless of whether you're trying to inform or persuade your boss, it's important to avoid making too many inflated claims or assertions without proof. In an effort to showcase your early progress as a manager or to curry favor with your boss, you may wind up exaggerating your team's accomplishments or setting unrealistically high expectations.

While bold, blustery comments can help you come across as a confident leader, such cockiness can come back to haunt you over the long term if your boss loses faith in what you say. As a new manager, preserving and strengthening your credibility should guide your upward communication.

Here are three traps you can fall into when speaking with your boss:

1. Evasion. In your first few months as a manager, you probably want to minimize the amount of bad news you must deliver to your boss. You also want to avoid too many "I don't know" answers, for fear of appearing ignorant or unprepared. So you wind up playing the evasion game, bobbing and weaving so that you don't have to say anything unpleasant, admit your lack of knowledge, or divulge troubling information about your unit's performance.

Evasion may buy you time, but it doesn't offer much of a solution. Indeed, most bosses will see through your hesitance to answer their questions head-on. They want the most valuable currency—timely information—and if you withhold it, they will lose trust in you.

2. The fact-opinion blur. Now that you're a manager, you may think that your opinions suddenly carry more weight. The result: when you chat with your boss, you feel free to let the dogmatic comments fly. You figure that one of the perks of power is not having to substantiate what you say. You can make predictions and label your staff with impunity, right?

Wrong. Bosses can tell when inexperienced supervisors state opinions that are disguised as facts. I call this "the fact-opinion blur." There's nothing wrong with occasionally offering your views, but if you state them as if they're self-evident truths, you risk sounding arrogant. And most bosses hate to manage know-it-alls.

3. Playing telephone. If you're going to serve as your boss's eyes and ears, make sure you're accurate. Alerting your boss to rumors or passing along tidbits of unconfirmed data can backfire if it turns out you're mistaken.

TRICKS OF THE TRADE

SPEAKING FOR THE RECORD
Improve your upward communication by inserting lots of "according-to statements." This means attributing a fact or observation to the proper source so that your boss can assess its reliability. Example: "Our retention rate is up 7 percent year-to-date, according to a report I requested from Ralph Smith in marketing."

Managing your upward communication is like playing "telephone," where each participant whispers a message to the next person. By the time the message travels from the first sender to the last receiver, it has been greatly distorted.

Caught in the Middle

Managing a boss is easy when everything goes well. But during a crisis, tensions can rise as tempers flare. That's when individuals let slip the kind of unfortunate comments that leave lasting scars.

The most difficult situations arise when rookie managers struggle to satisfy angry employees while complying with the boss's controversial orders. I met a foreman at a manufacturing facility who had to decide after only three weeks on the job whether to follow his boss's direction to turn off the air-conditioning on the factory floor—or leave it on to make the workplace bearable for his laborers.

Looking worried and worn, he called it a "lose-lose deal." If he indulged his boss's command to shut off the air-conditioning, his employees would surely rebel (or simply quit). If he rejected the order, he risked punishment for insubordination.

He couldn't decide what to do. Finally, when his boss asked how the workers had responded to the lack of air-conditioning, the beleaguered foreman blurted out, "The real question is why they don't walk out of this hellhole. I ask myself the same thing sometimes." Naturally, the boss blew up at the foreman's snide remark. Their relationship only worsened after that, until the foreman agreed to resign a few months later.

What the foreman should have done—aside from controlling his emotions and unleashing his frustrations in a more productive manner—was to ask his boss the reasons for the order. Had he done so, he would have learned that his boss was under extreme pressure from the president to cut costs. Armed with this insight, the foreman could have proposed other measures to reduce operating expenses and even relayed some sensible money-saving suggestions that his crew had mentioned to him.

Even if he couldn't come up with any better ideas to cut costs, asking his boss for the rationale for such an unpopular move would at least help him explain it to his employees. Instead, he was left shrugging and rolling his eyes when his furious workers demanded to know why the "bigwigs at this place don't want us to have air-conditioning."

THE MANAGER AS CONDUIT

When you pass along an order from your boss that you know will trigger an outcry from the troops, follow this three-step procedure. First, explain the order in clear, neutral language. Don't reveal contempt for the boss or otherwise criticize or mock the boss when you discuss the directive with employees. Second, **TOOLS** reinforce a larger goal, such as the organization's need to survive a business downturn or the importance of making collective sacrifices to facilitate teamwork and increase long-term job security for everyone. Finally, reserve time for questions. Don't just tell workers what they must do; let them vent and listen patiently to their concerns.

In many cases, it's wise to tell a boss that you disagree with an order. But don't magnify the situation by pretending it's a life-or-death matter. Use phrases such as "Another strategy that strikes me as more appealing is . . ." or "As much as I disagree with that, I understand what you're trying to do." Speak in a pleasant tone; don't overdramatize your remarks. Conclude by reassuring your boss that, despite your misgivings, you will comply with the instruction to the best of your ability. (Of course, if you're asked to break a work rule or behave unethically, you're justified in refusing to comply.)

At some point, almost every new manager gets caught in the middle. You're not alone. Treat this as another aspect of the job that you need to manage, not as a drop-dead crisis. Realize that every boss looks like an idiot or makes unreasonable demands on occasion, and you must choose the most appropriate, professional response.

Pick the Right Personality

Be yourself.

That's fine advice if you're on a first date, trying to hit it off and make sparks fly. But to manage your boss, your natural personality may work for or against you.

ADJUST TO FIT

Managing up gets difficult if your unbendable personality clashes with your boss's personality. It's better to bend a little. Indra Nooyi, PepsiCo's CEO, has said that she wakes up at night, grabs some paper, and strategizes about the company. If you report to someone like her, embrace strategic thinking even if it doesn't come naturally to you. Or if you report to a combative executive who enjoys picking verbal fights, tweak your normally placid personality so that you're occasionally aggressive and even confrontational.

New managers may embody one of four personality types. A mismatch between your personality and your boss's personality can almost guarantee that conflicts will erupt.

Deniers turn away from unpleasantness. They deny harsh reality. They figure, "If I don't think about it, it'll go away on its own." These managers may withhold their concerns from their boss or sugarcoat a serious problem because they don't have the stomach to confront it head-on. What's worse, they may convince themselves over time that no problems exist.

If you're a denier, then you'd better hope you have an equally oblivious boss. If both of you agree to disregard certain issues or pretend that everything's fine, then you can proceed without fear of punishment. Crises won't disappear, of course, but at least you'll have the support from above to manage them by ignoring them.

Jokesters use humor as their favorite coping mechanism. Even if they're in over their heads, they crack jokes and keep smiling. They may resort to harmless puns, good-natured riddles, or even minor pranks to dispel tension around the office. Or they may regale listeners (including their bosses) with long stories that deliver only questionably funny punch lines.

Some rookie managers resort to gallows humor to describe their experience. I've heard newly minted managers refer to themselves as "prisoners of war" or "Death Row inmates" because they feel trapped in a position that offers no peace or escape. While some bosses may find such talk offensive, such as an executive who knows first-

> ### HIDING THE TRUTH
>
> **CAUTION**
>
> In the early months of establishing a relationship with a new boss, beware of denying or brushing away potential problems. You may prefer to compartmentalize and block off certain areas, but the boss may misinterpret your refusal to deal with certain issues as a stubbornness or weakness to fix what's broken. Listen to your boss's concerns and acknowledge them. Raise some of your own, too. Show that you're willing to analyze even the most thorny parts of your job dispassionately and hash out solutions.

hand what it's like fighting a war, others may indulge a jokester and even try to top the new manager by volleying back more witticisms.

> ### CUTTING THE WISECRACKS
>
> **FOR EXAMPLE**
>
> Jan loved to joke around. When she became a manager, she figured her brand of humor would endear her to her staff and her boss, Karen. While her employees liked her witty nature, Karen viewed Jan as a lightweight. Karen thought that Jan's constant need to crack jokes was a weakness, indicating that she couldn't take things seriously. What's more, Karen rarely laughed. Jan realized she needed to adjust her personality to build a better rapport with Karen, so she made an effort to mimic Karen's communication style: straightforward, precise, and humorless. Karen began to like and trust Jan, and Jan eventually loosened up again—but only when she could use her humor to provide a welcome relief.

If you use humor as your first line of defense against assorted challenges, make sure your boss appreciates—or at least tolerates—your behavior. Watch how she acts when you tell jokes. If you're greeted with a blank face or even a dash of annoyance or impatience, that's a sure sign you should cut the mirth and focus more intently on serious matters.

Worriers always seem discouraged or overwhelmed. And most bosses dread having to manage them.

If you tend to fret over every decision or habitually talk about your ever-mounting anxieties, consider the effect that has on your boss. You'll hardly build your boss's confidence in your management; in fact, you may needlessly undermine your image by coming across as a sky-is-falling pessimist.

Ironically, many worriers are actually competent managers. Their fretful nature may disguise their determination to tackle multiple tasks well. But their bosses may conclude that these managers simply lack the poise and inner strength to persevere during tough times.

"I've got a new manager who pushes the panic button every day," a vice president of human resources told me. "She is always on edge, worrying about stuff that doesn't merit even a second of thought. It's too bad, because it really limits her effectiveness."

If you're a worrier, then it will almost definitely work against you if you want to build rapport with your boss. Unless you're "lucky" enough to report to someone who's also a stress monger—in which case the two of you may work yourselves into a tizzy together—then you're better off venting your anxieties outside of work in a safe manner. Help your boss see you as a strong, sturdy manager who won't crumble under pressure.

Impulsives have short attention spans. They will talk without thinking, resulting in frequent bouts of foot-in-mouth disease. Impulsives also wind up putting out fires all day, because they do not plan or take preventive steps to avoid blow-ups down the line.

Some bosses enjoy managing impulsives for their shoot-from-the-hip honesty. But if you're a new manager with an impulsive personality, don't count on having a receptive boss. If you're easily daunted by the prospect of plotting a strategy and then implementing it slowly in stages, then you may drive your higher-ups crazy.

Many bosses conclude that impulsives are actually lazy. They may figure that if you don't like to think through what you're going to do before you plunge in, then you're simply undisciplined, disorganized, or both. You won't stand a chance of getting ahead if you continue to act impulsively with a disapproving boss.

Instead, force yourself to explain how you're going to tackle a project. Get in the habit of breaking an assignment into numbered steps—and

> ### FOLLOW A "TWO-SECOND CLOCK"
> **SMART**
>
> **MANAGING**
>
> If you tend to blurt whatever's on your mind, you may let slip comments that your boss finds silly, insulting, or incorrect. You need to tame your impulsive side. Here's how: when talking with your boss, mentally count to two before you speak. This applies whether you're responding to a question or making a statement. Then, after completing your point, stop talking. Some impulsives will add to what they've said with spontaneous asides that prove needless and distracting.

then telling your boss how you've designed a "three-step process" or a "two-prong attack to this problem." This shows that you're not jumping right into a task, and it proves you're able to control your impulsiveness when it counts.

The Magic of "Underpromise/Overdeliver"

The best way to manage your boss is to manage your boss's expectations. By consistently producing *more* work and *better* results than your boss has any reason to anticipate, you'll stand out as an exceptional new manager.

The trick to setting the right expectations involves two steps. First, initiate projects that'll have a direct bottom-line impact. Second define how you'll track your progress. Don't wait for your superiors to tell you what to do.

Say you want to enact reforms to increase the responsiveness of your firm's customer service. You write a three-part memo to your boss outlining your goal, an action

> ### WHY WAIT?
>
> **FOR EXAMPLE**
>
> Karen Schaffer, president of MicroArts Creative Agency in Greenland, New Hampshire, spent three years at the firm before earning a promotion to president. She told me that she impressed her boss by "not waiting to be asked to do something." Her proactive attitude led her to initiate steps to generate more business and find new ways to produce results for existing clients.

plan to meet it, and a timetable for producing results. But don't commit to stretch goals in writing. Make sure to set realistic objectives that you're sure you can meet—and exceed. That way, you leave your boss even more impressed with your performance.

Same goes when you're discussing a project face-to-face with your boss. Resist the urge to commit to something you're not absolutely sure you can deliver. It's better to set the bar lower at the outset and raise it as you go along.

In weighing what kind of goals you should set, consider your boss's frame of reference. The only way to ensure that you underpromise and overdeliver is if you take the time to understand how your boss perceives the situation. Ask yourself these questions first:

- Do I know how my boss is held accountable by his bosses? What measurements do they use to evaluate his success?
- What pressures does my boss face?
- How does my boss track my work performance?
- What does my boss expect from me? What would it take for me to exceed those expectations?
- To what extent will my boss notice or care if I exceed expectations? What steps can I take to call attention to my results?

If your boss pushes you beyond your limits and sets absurdly high expectations, then underpromising and overdelivering may seem impossible. But it's not. That's because you should not accept the boss's goals blindly. Instead, explain the basis for your more realistic expectations. Then add, "I like the challenge you've laid out. I'm not going to promise you what I can't deliver, but I can promise you'll get 100 percent from me all the time." That way, you set the stage to delight your boss by proving you can push yourself farther than you thought you could go.

Giving Progress Reports

Bosses love information.

The more you can furnish them with the latest numbers—from weekly sales and expenses to historical trends (such as month-to-month results)—the more comfortable they'll feel both in assessing your performance and relaying the numbers to their higher-ups. By tracking the same hard data, you also prove that you're thinking like a senior executive. That builds your credibility.

Soon after you become a manager, ask your boss what key ratios or benchmarks matter most in your unit. Confirm how you can compute these numbers accurately, and make sure you have access to the necessary information. For example, a new underwriting manager at an insurance company may be held accountable for maintaining a low "loss ratio" (how insurance executives calculate how much money the company collects versus the amount paid in claims to policyholders). A manager would want to arrange for daily updates on the loss ratio to avoid surprises—and angry

> **A MENU OF CHOICES** TRICKS OF THE TRADE
>
> Manage your boss more effectively by listing all the gauges you use to measure your unit's performance. Examples might include sales per employee, turnover rate, customer complaints, click-through rates on online advertising, etc. Then ask your boss to rank all the measures in order of importance or relevance in assessing you and your team. Armed with this information, you ensure that your progress reports will serve a valuable purpose in giving the boss exactly what he or she needs.

bosses bursting in and demanding answers for poor results.

Invite your boss to tell you the best way to communicate your unit's performance. Don't assume that because you like to chat face-to-face, so does your manager. Many executives prefer to scan financial reports and want to receive such information either online or in management meetings. Anne Wojcicki, cofounder of 23andMe, a genetic testing firm in Mountain View, California, likes to host weekly strategy sessions with her senior managers. "My goal is to check on things like sales figures and our budget versus the burn [rate]," she told *Inc.* magazine in 2012.

When giving updates to higher-ups, don't dwell on what's going well and hype your wise decisions. The real test of your boss management skills comes when you acknowledge poor results or admit errors. It's understandable to show reluctance in confessing missed targets, blown opportunities, or careless blunders. But that's no excuse to bury the bad news.

New managers may try to let slip the disappointing news in between lots of "happy talk." That's usually a mistake. Nothing irritates a boss more than having someone introduce a gloomy note into an otherwise upbeat conversation. It's better to wait for a moment when you're both in neutral business mode, reviewing the organization's goals and analyzing the latest numbers. That way, you can tie your message to bottom-line concerns and present a solution that'll make the bad news easier to swallow.

Show a willingness to take responsibility for setbacks, even if you're not personally at fault. Most bosses appreciate having an honest, straightforward manager who doesn't shift blame when problems erupt. When you say, "This happened on my watch, so I take responsibility," chances are your boss will insist that you not take it so hard. And that's exactly the kind of relationship you want to establish.

New Manager's Checklist for Chapter 11

☑ When communicating with your boss, avoid groundless claims or assertions without proof. Instead, amass plenty of facts to support your position.

☑ Beware of stating your opinions as facts. Bosses often see through this, and it can raise their suspicions.

☑ When relaying your boss's unpopular orders to your staff, explain the orders in clear, neutral language. Then reinforce a larger organizational goal, and leave time for questions.

☑ Disagree with your boss without overdramatizing it. Point out how your view differs and provide evidence to support your position.

☑ Don't boast to your boss about how you intend to exceed even the most ambitious performance goals. Instead, underpromise and overdeliver.

☑ Learn how your boss prefers to absorb information and review your progress. Identify the key ratios or numbers that drive your unit's performance and track the same data.

Cultivating a Network

t's lonely at the top. At least that's what some fast-rising managers say when they no longer can open up with their coworkers. Now that these managers wield authority, they have to watch what they say and cut their griping. They're often isolated from people whom they can trust, especially when they're uncomfortable chatting with their boss.

Yet it doesn't have to come to this. You can ascend into management ranks without severing all ties with your former coworkers. And with some aggressive networking, you can use your new job to open doors that provide access to a whole new cast of high-powered characters.

Maximize Social Media

Managers looking to network take steps to raise their profile, especially online. They cultivate friends using popular sites such as Facebook and Twitter, but they also build visibility on more targeted sites such as LinkedIn.com and Ryze.com.

The site that has come to dominate business networking is LinkedIn. With nearly 200 million members, LinkedIn has attained such scale that it's tough to ignore. It is gaining two new members per second.

Treat LinkedIn as a self-marketing tool—a way to advance your career goals by promoting your strengths. Begin by becoming a member and choosing keywords to describe your skills and credentials, including industry processes or software you've mastered, equipment you've used, and professional designations you've earned. Use Google AdWords Keyword Tool to select the most popular search terms.

In your LinkedIn profile, list highlights of your work experience rather than a full résumé. Inject specifics that differentiate you from other managers. Replace "An insurance risk manager with a decade of experience" with "A 10-year insurance risk manager with expertise in spotting trends, conducting fleet vehicle safety inspections, and creating value."

Online networking doesn't just happen on its own; you need to initiate it and stay involved. Recommend colleagues whose work you admire. Vouch for vendors who deliver as promised. Your testimonials not only solidify your relationships with those you endorse, but the testimonials also underscore your professionalism and give others a sense of what you do and what you're like as a person.

REVEAL ONLY WHAT ENHANCES YOUR PROFESSIONAL IMAGE

CAUTION

On professional social media sites such as LinkedIn, treat every photo you download and every word you write as a permanent addition to your online image. You're crafting your reputation. Don't blow it by blurring the line between personal antics and professional news. Remember that any employer, employee, client, or acquaintance can access your online profile. Make sure they see only what you want them to see.

As you'll soon discover, LinkedIn is inclusive. From administrative assistants to midlevel managers to senior executives, everyone's participating. A 2012 survey by CEO.com found that 129 CEOs of Fortune 500 firms had LinkedIn profiles (and 19 CEOs registered for Twitter and 38 were on Facebook). Your network will grow in all directions if you expend the effort.

Once you join LinkedIn, stay active. Devote at least an hour a week reaching out to your network. Share your latest projects, slides from your presentations, or your views on industry developments. And comment on others' activity, expressing praise and encouragement when appropriate.

ORGANIZATIONS CAN NETWORK, TOO

SMART

MANAGING

Along with your own networking needs, consider how you can help your employer with its networking needs. LinkedIn enables organizations to share photos, brand images, and thought leader content. Companies can present detailed information on products and services, with frequent status updates on mergers and acquisitions, community outreach, or geographic expansion. Look for ways to contribute to your employer's online activities and initiatives. It's one more way for you to meet colleagues—and help them succeed.

With the growth of Twitter, some new managers find themselves charged with overseeing a Twitter account for their business unit. Increasingly, companies are using these accounts to reach potential customers in a particular market. Before you tweet, review your employer's social media policies so that you understand how to identify and engage your target audience.

You'll need to distinguish between using Twitter to advance corporate goals (such as reinforcing your organization's advertising campaign) and using it to expand your network. There's a big difference. Know your objective and maintain consistent messaging. If you seek to use Twitter to build your organization's brand, for instance, stick to brand-related messages and avoid personal disclosure or reflections about your current job or career goals.

Networking via Twitter can work to your advantage, as long as you honor your employer's social media policies and use your tweets to establish yourself as a knowledgeable professional. You can showcase your expertise and intelligence by sharing trenchant observations about your industry and stating insightful, diplomatically worded opinions.

A TWEET THAT ROARS

FOR EXAMPLE

Greg Sandoval used Twitter to build his personal network, commenting frequently about the digital music business. In January 2013, he was an editor at CNET, a respected technology news website, when he announced his resignation via a tweet. The reason? He objected to CNET's parent company, CBS Corp., for its apparent attempt to exert undue influence over CNET's editorial content. Sandoval's public resignation struck a nerve: Hundreds retweeted his announcement and praised his integrity. He even received several job offers.

Enliven Your Presence

To expand your circle of corporate friends and acquaintances, it's important to sharpen your professional presence. If you radiate confidence, you'll draw people to you. But if you appear anxious, forlorn, or constantly distracted, others will steer clear of engaging in conversation with you.

DO YOU PUSH PEOPLE AWAY OR PULL 'EM IN?

CAUTION

While there are dozens of ways to erect barriers that sabotage your face-to-face networking, here are the five biggest mistakes you can make: frown or sigh when you meet people, talk too much about yourself, fail to ask questions, refuse to approach others, and listen halfheartedly. By greeting people with a smile, showing interest in them, and retaining everything they say, you'll maximize every encounter.

Establishing a professional presence involves a complex set of variables. You want to attract just the right amount of positive attention, like an intriguing and appealing package in a store—without going overboard. And you want to put people at ease.

Don't get caught up in trivia. How you dress doesn't really matter as much as how you express yourself. As long as you aren't decked out in glaringly inappropriate clothing, then the fact that your pants are a quarter-inch too long or you have a slight stain on your shirt collar won't matter. Yet your facial expression, posture, and willingness to launch conversations *do* matter. You need to make others believe you enjoy talking with them. By welcoming opportunities to meet and greet people—rather than avoiding them—you'll become a much more productive and formidable networker.

Make the First Minute Count

You don't need to attend conferences or trade group meetings to network. As a new manager, you have a perfect opportunity to introduce yourself to colleagues throughout your organization. And the more contacts you can forge at your company, the greater your chances of making friends in high places, monitoring the rumor mill, and learning about functions or departments other than your own.

It all begins with a pleasant greeting and an outstretched hand. Turning to a stranger in the elevator and saying, "Hi, I'm Chris Jones" can only work to your advantage. At best, you can get to know someone who will make your new management job easier. At worst, your five-second investment of time will not pay off as the conversation sputters to a halt. Even then, however, there's no harm done.

OPENING LINES

To ease into conversations with strangers, prepare a few all-purpose icebreakers. Before saying "Hello, I'm ...," you may prefer to preface your remarks with a friendly comment such as "I should introduce myself." Once you get past the introduction, be ready to carry the dialogue forward. Here's a good follow-up line: "I'm a new manager in the _____ department." Explaining your role almost guarantees that the other person will say something at least somewhat interesting or relevant to you. Another example: "I notice that you're carrying/wearing/working on ...." Using your observational skills to spark a more lively, personal exchange can work well if you want to learn more about someone.

TRICKS OF THE TRADE

Soon after striking up a conversation, you may find yourself fighting off a host of nagging irritants. For instance, your initial negative judgment of another person may cloud your ability to listen with an open mind. This can happen as soon as you hear someone's voice, which may have an accent you dislike or a cold, stern tone you find objectionable. Or you may find yourself trapped with a motormouth who monopolizes your time as you seek an escape. What's worse, you may grow so self-conscious that you neglect to pay attention. Any traces of insecurity can intensify if you sense the other person finds you somehow off-putting.

To test whether you're in the right frame of mind to network successfully, monitor your thoughts as the conversation begins. Ideally, you should focus on:

- Learning more
- Making the other person feel comfortable
- Expressing genuine enthusiasm for the chance to get to know each other

On the other hand, if your mind wanders and you ponder any of these thoughts, you're already digging yourself into a hole:

- I look terrible today.
- I'm not in the mood to continue this.
- I don't like this person.

The surest way to sabotage your networking is to prejudge others. Based on someone's attitude or appearance, you may figure it's not worth the effort to introduce yourself. Or perhaps you've heard damning statements about this person through the grapevine, so you avoid as much as a simple hello.

Even if you rise above these concerns and try to chat, you may not treat certain individuals as openly if you perceive them as tainted. Banish all negative judgments from your mind when you launch a conversation.

FOR EXAMPLE

A New Beginning

When Warren became a manager, he decided that he needed to expand his network throughout the five-floor corporate headquarters where he worked. So whenever he saw a familiar face in the hallway, parking lot, or cafeteria, he'd say, "I've seen you around. I want to introduce myself. I'm Warren, and I just started as a manager in the electronics unit." In some cases, people didn't warm up right away. They gave a perfunctory response that hurt Warren's feelings. But he persevered, doing this so many times that it became automatic. After approaching 10 or so people, he no longer took it personally if they didn't seem friendly. He just kept them talking until they could establish at least some rapport.

Radiate enthusiasm with your body language when you first meet someone. Give a firm handshake while standing up straight with your weight balanced evenly on both feet. Don't tilt your head to one side or start talking with downcast eyes. Look directly at the person. Try to communicate warmth and goodwill with pleasant facial expressions and open, welcoming gestures. The best networkers put people at ease from the outset, and that makes the conversation flow more smoothly.

Tracking Your Progress

As you're probably discovering, almost every aspect of managing involves the use of systems, processes, and record keeping. Many new managers find that they've never before kept track of so much information—or had so many ways to analyze it.

Same goes with networking. If you want to make more contacts and ensure that you're in the loop, you can't leave it to chance or allow your mood to dictate when you feel like meeting new people. Instead, set a goal of establishing a set number of new acquaintances every week, whether through online or face-to-face networking.

For example, say you decide you want to add at least five individuals to your network every week. You work at a small company, so networking internally isn't necessary. That means you need to seek out new contacts by asking yourself, "Whom do I want to get to know?" You conclude it's best to befriend customers, vendors, suppliers, and even some managers who work at rival firms. And don't neglect consultants who work on projects for your organization: get their business cards and follow up with an e-mail in which you offer to serve as a resource.

The next step is to log your results. Tally every networking encounter in a secure file on your computer or a notebook that you carry with you all day. Divide the page into three columns with the headings "Who," "Topics Discussed," and "Commitments." Soon after you part ways with someone you've just met, you can fill in the blanks.

You may think it's strange or inappropriate to keep such formal records of your informal chats. But it serves a purpose. By keeping count and retaining what others tell you

> **CAPTURE THOSE DETAILS!** **SMART**
>
> When tracking your networking, pay special attention to recording the "Topics Discussed." Rather than describe **MANAGING** the conversation in vague terms such as "talked shop" or "compared notes," be specific. For example, write "analyzed disaster recovery plans" or "shared new product rollout strategy." Also confirm the spelling of the person's full name in the "Who" column. Finally, when you tell someone you'll "try" to do something rather than promise to do it, you may still want to jot that down in the "Commitments" column. This will prod you to follow through.

by writing it down, you hold yourself more accountable. If you set a goal of adding five people to your network every week, then you will know at a glance how you're doing. And your fleeting mood swings or fears of rejection or embarrassment won't stop you if you're determined to reach your weekly objective.

In some cases, you can network in real time. When you meet people who suggest that you read a certain book or check out a website, reach for your handheld device or a pen and pad and say, "Give me a moment. I want to send myself a reminder." The benefit is twofold: the speaker will appreciate that you clearly intend to follow up and you won't have to risk forgetting these facts later.

If you want to learn even more from your record keeping, then chart your week-to-week progress. Every Friday afternoon, count the number of contacts you've made. Then graph the results. Within a few months, you'll begin to easily spot any dips or surges in your networking activity. This can help you identify the challenges that can block your outreach efforts, such as falling behind during the last week of every month when you're facing deadlines. Armed with this awareness, you can take steps to maintain your networking pace despite such obstacles.

Who Knows About You?

You're now a manager, but that doesn't mean everyone in your organization knows about it. When you walk down the hall, there's no sign around your neck that reads, "I was just promoted to manager!" Unless you're suddenly dressing differently or your office now resides in the executive suite, casual observers may have no way of understanding your new role. It's up to you to spread the word, without overdoing it.

If your boss sends a mass e-mail announcing your promotion, don't assume everyone will read it. Many new managers tell me they're dispirited by how few people know or care about their happy news.

But you need not rely on your boss or the folks in Human Resources to compose a snappy memo to alert your colleagues about your promotion. You can toot your own horn—and network successfully at the same time. Here are three ways to do it:

1. **Query your company.** Through crowdsourcing, researchers who seek information on an obscure topic can use the Internet to invite experts to share their knowledge, thus turning thousands of strangers into potential research assistants. You can borrow this tactic to make contacts in your organization. Many organizations have an intranet or an internal "wiki" where employees can share ideas

and pool their know-how. Write an online query explaining a project you're working on and asking for help, such as seeking volunteers for a cross-departmental team. Mention your new position as manager and the project's benefits and bottom-line impact to the organization. This is a relatively painless way to network, because respondents will ultimately come to you. And your coworkers can become valuable sources of information to help you do your job better.

2. **Make the rounds.** Contact department heads and offer to serve as a guest speaker at their staff meetings. Invite colleagues in other parts of the firm to luncheons or award ceremonies with your employees. The more you break down barriers between units of your organization, the easier you can mingle with people in other departments.

3. **Join cross-departmental teams.** One of the most effortless ways to network is to get yourself named to groups that collaborate on big projects. By contributing your expertise to the team, you can earn the respect of influential executives whom you would never otherwise meet.

When you attend company events, such as a picnic or a training seminar, don't cling to coworkers. Strike up conversations with the person sitting next to you in class or standing behind you in line in the cafeteria. Even if you only commiserate about the bad weather or the exploits of your local sports teams, that's enough to get you started. The next time you see that person, you can build on your prior contact.

Fighting Off Fears

Let me guess: you're buried in work, trying to make sense of your new job as manager. You know it's a good idea to network, but you don't have the time.

That's no excuse.

The process of meeting people both inside and outside your organization is imperative to your career advancement. Plus, you never know what you'll learn by initiating contact with a variety of professionals.

Even if you see the value of networking, you may conclude you're too anxious or scared. Fear can let you off the hook.

Unless you're a natural extrovert, you may prefer to keep a low profile and limit your small talk with strangers. That's the easy way out, and it comes at a price: you'll limit your effectiveness as a manager. You'll isolate yourself and lack allies when you need them.

If the thought of introducing yourself to people rattles you, then conquer your fears. You need to move outside your comfort zone so that you take risks and increase the number of "cold chats" that you initiate. The more conversations you launch with people you don't know, the more doors will open for you and the more insights you'll collect to improve how you manage.

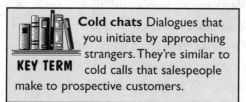

Cold chats Dialogues that you initiate by approaching strangers. They're similar to

KEY TERM cold calls that salespeople make to prospective customers.

If you're reluctant to network more aggressively even though you know it's a wise idea, you're probably succumbing to some mild if not severe fears. Once you expose these anxieties and develop strategies to overcome them, you can proceed with more confidence.

Here are three of the most common fears that may inhibit you:

1. **Fear of embarrassment.** When initiating a conversation with someone you don't know, your mind can play tricks on you. Rather than enjoying the moment, you may convince yourself that you'll suffer foot-in-mouth disease and say something stupid. Or you may worry about your appearance so much that you don't bother to listen. If you're preoccupied with such distractions, you'll speak haltingly and appear frazzled and jittery. Replace these thoughts of self-sabotage with mental messages that reinforce your eagerness to listen and learn. Realize that the way you carry yourself matters far more than if your lipstick is fading or your tie is crooked.

I'm Losing It!

CAUTION When networking, don't dwell on whether you're losing face or embarrassing yourself. If you're unhappy with your appearance or you let slip a remark that you instantly regret, plow onward. Banish doubts such as "I look terrible today" or "I sure sounded dumb saying that" or "I think I just insulted him by mistake." You'll bounce back more quickly from any bouts of embarrassment if you persevere and continue to breathe life into the conversation.

2. **Fear of rejection.** You're on a high now that you've been promoted into management. The last thing you want to do is jeopardize your heightened sense of worth by entering into conversations with people who look down on you or seem to dismiss you. The result is you avoid placing yourself at risk of being rejected. There's a reason almost everyone fears rejection: it happens to almost everyone. And it hurts. But consider the odds. If you launch 10 cold chats a week with both outsiders and colleagues within your organization, one (or maybe two on a really bad week) may lead to rejection. The other person might respond to your friendliness by withdrawing in a huff or making snide or condescending comments. But it's a numbers game. There's no reason to fear rejection if you keep plowing away and networking with more people. Some setbacks come with the territory, but they shouldn't stop you from making progress.

3. **Fear of boredom.** Your time is money. You have a full agenda. You find most people you meet are intolerable bores. You conclude that stopping to chat in the hall or on your way to the taxi stand after a conference is a big waste. The chance that you'll get trapped with a loudmouth or a braggart is enough to keep you from saying hello. You've had your share of one-way encounters where you yearned to escape, and that's one of the reasons you hate to network. But the solution isn't to give in to your fear. Rather, try to awaken your curiosity and learn from even the most annoying or talkative people. Give them a chance to stir your interest. Don't say to yourself, "I'm bored and trapped" after only 30 seconds. Suspend your judgment until a few minutes have passed and you give yourself a fair chance to extract some valuable piece of information from the speaker.

Mingling with Outsiders

Now that you're a manager, you will probably attend more training programs, conferences, and other networking events. This enables you to expand your list of contacts both inside and outside your industry. But it also means mingling with nosy outsiders who may take advantage of your openness to extract valuable information.

While you should forge relationships with people you like and respect, networking with outsiders can backfire if you reveal proprietary information or get too cozy with the competition. In your eagerness to gain acceptance, you may tell others about your company's growth plans and how you fit in. Or you may wind up giving negative opinions about a notorious bigwig in your industry—only to learn that they admire the individual you loathe.

In any networking situation, it's wise to ask great questions and get others to do most of the talking. That's even more important when you're meeting outsiders. You can't say something you regret later if you keep quiet for most of the conversation.

Another danger of networking with people outside your organization is that they'll try to "top" you. They may want to reinforce their own self-importance by showing off how much more power or influence they exert at their company, or how much more experience or expertise they possess. Yet by speaking in a polite, engaging tone, they still come across as easy to talk to rather than obnoxious blowhards.

> **TRICKS OF THE TRADE**
>
> ## HERE'S MY ANSWER
>
> Don't feel obliged to answer every question you're asked. You can make friends without blindly supplying whatever information others request. If a competitor wants to know your unit's gross sales or the status of some litigation involving your firm, don't blurt out an answer. Instead, ask a question in return such as "Why are you curious about that?" Remain pleasant but vigilant. Volley back questions, and you'll keep a conversation lively—without getting yourself in trouble.

Don't take offense too quickly if someone contradicts you or tries to upstage you. Successful networkers give strangers the benefit of the doubt—at least once. Rise above your initial judgments so that you can get to know someone better. If after 10 minutes it's clear you're dealing with a nonstop braggart, then call it quits.

In many cases, however, you can forge bonds with others by bypassing their faults and letting them showcase their good side. Keep them talking and resist sweeping indictments of their character. Above all, don't rush to disagree with what you hear or you'll put people on the defensive. Stay neutral in the first few minutes to make your networking pay off.

Also beware of turning your networking chats into gripe sessions.

Never complain too much about your job to a stranger. The person sitting next to you at a seminar may know your boss and relay everything you said. As a test, only say to an outsider what you would say to an insider at your organization. Or imagine that everything you say is being piped into your boss's office. That should remind you to use discretion.

CITE YOUR SOURCE, PLEASE

SMART MANAGING

Nothing kills a networking encounter as much as contradiction. If you think you hear a misstatement or an inaccurate fact, don't say, "That's wrong" and offer an instant correction. Instead, challenge others with a question such as "How did you arrive at that?" Or in a curious, friendly tone, cite a source that clashes with what they said, "That's funny. The *Wall Street Journal* reported something different last week."

Finally, never network out of desperation. Too much neediness is a turnoff. Say you've decided you want a new job. You meet a hiring executive at a firm where you'd love to work. Rather than engage in genial, nonthreatening conversation by asking smart, stimulating questions, you come on strong and almost beg for help. The more you push, the more the executive pulls away.

Greet outsiders with enthusiasm, but don't overdo it. If you want something from them, keep it to yourself during the first few minutes as you get to know each other. Let your request arise naturally from the conversation. Ideally, you want them to ask you if there's anything they can

RAINMAKING IN ACTION

FOR EXAMPLE

When Jim became a manager, his boss told him that he was now expected to bring more business to the firm. So Jim refined his networking skills in an effort to become a "rainmaker"—a key contact who could attract wealthy clients. Jim attended industry conferences and approached attendees by asking, "What brings you here?" Most of them would volunteer their needs, such as seeking ways to manage change better or comply with ever-changing employment laws. Jim would ask more questions, but before each follow-up question he inserted one statement such as "My other clients say the same thing" or "That's funny, because my firm solves those kind of problems for our clients." Soon the people he met grew so curious that they started asking Jim about his firm's services.

do to assist you. And the best way to make that happen is to look for opportunities to do something to help them, from giving them a book you think they'd enjoy to forwarding them a business article on a topic they care about. Meanwhile, shower them with attention, keep them talking, and forge bonds by finding common cause or highlighting shared perspectives.

New Manager's Checklist for Chapter 12

☑ Harness social media to expand your network.

☑ Introduce yourself without fanfare. Extend your hand and say, "Hi, I'm . . . ." You don't need a fancy opening line.

☑ Ask lots of questions. Look for opportunities to express genuine enthusiasm at the answers.

☑ Keep a log of your networking activity. Note key details you hear and commitments either party makes.

☑ Raise your visibility at your organization by networking aggressively. Offer to join cross-departmental teams, speak to other units, and ask advice.

☑ Fight off fears of networking by confronting them head-on. Acknowledge your anxieties and examine why they inhibit you.

☑ Watch what you say when meeting outsiders. Don't reveal too much about your employer. Ask more questions than you answer.

Leading Teams to Triumph

N ew managers can be so naive. They may assume all it takes to get people to work together is to give them a clear goal, express faith in their ability to collaborate, and dangle the right reward if they succeed.

Sadly, it's never that easy.

Giving teams a concrete objective is a necessary starting point, of course. People must understand what they're supposed to do and why it matters to the organization.

Praising the team can't hurt either. Buttering them up by saying, "You're the best" and "I couldn't be prouder to have such an all-star group here" might endear you to them and pump up their spirits a bit.

Incentives and celebrations play a role as well. Teams like to know what's to gain if and when they deliver the results you seek.

Yet there's so much more that new managers need to know about group dynamics if they're going to maximize their use of teams, foster collaboration, and create an environment where individuals sacrifice a chance to bask in their own glory for the betterment of the group.

If you ask seasoned managers to reflect on lessons learned about leading teams, you'll probably hear answers such as:

- "Recruit the right mix of personalities and competencies. You want most everyone to be compatible or at least not divisive. And you want

MY NEEDS—OR YOUR INTERESTS?

CAUTION

Just because you form a team and urge everyone to pull together to achieve a vital goal for the organization does not assure employees will buy in. It's not enough to ask yourself, "What do *I* need this team to do?" Instead, ask, "How can I appeal to the *shared interests of everyone* on the team so that they all care about contributing to a common goal?"

each person to bring expertise or experience that the group needs."

■ "Culture comes first. If you operate in a culture that prizes team achievement over individual achievement, you're halfway home."

■ "Communication drives team success. As the leader, you need to convey how the team's efforts will impact the bottom line. Make them see the stakes—and make sure you're talking about high stakes."

All of the above comments highlight critical aspects of team success. Picking people who feel honored or at least somewhat motivated to help the group advance toward its goal can limit the risk of unleashing an egomaniac to run amuck.

An organization that celebrates collective triumphs as part of a culture of teamwork makes any new manager's life easier. With that cultural backdrop, you can rally a group to succeed without worrying as much about glory hounds or saboteurs getting in the way.

Your communication skills can make or break a team. It's not just whether you articulate a clear goal at the outset. The real test comes once team members get to work. Are you guiding them to focus on what counts? Are you willing to listen to their complaints? Do you level with them when they're wasting time or harping on nonessentials?

As you'll learn in this chapter, leading teams really boils down to communicating well. Like so many other aspects of people management, the secret is stepping back and exerting leadership with dignity and quiet force.

Manage Your Message

Teams, like individuals, need direction. If you don't provide it, one of two things might happen (neither of them good). The group can become rudderless, aimlessly trying to figure out what to do with itself. Or the team can take its cue from someone else, perhaps a strong-willed member who proclaims, "This is what we must do." You may not like where this would-be leader takes the team.

To avoid such unwanted outcomes, step up and blaze a productive path for the group. Give it a purpose. Deliver simple, consistent messages to reinforce that purpose so that there's no way anyone can misunderstand or misinterpret what you want and why you've formed the team.

HIGH STAKES

TRICKS OF THE TRADE

In your first team meeting, summarize what's at stake. Say, "Let's fast-forward a few months and envision where we're at." Ideally, you want to peer into a crystal ball and help the group see the consequences of its actions. What will success look like? Perhaps the team's output or ideas will enable your company to mount a rebranding campaign or expand its customer base. If the team must identify austerity measures or cost-cutting moves, maybe the firm's very survival hangs in the balance. Define what's at stake and how it affects the organization's future.

Teams tend to expend more energy and collaborate more fully when participants feel like their work matters. Emphasize that they are embarking on a critical mission. Members are more likely to treat their involvement seriously if they detect heightened levels of interest in their work coming from you and other senior managers.

To prepare to deliver a resoundingly clear message at the team's first meeting, use these questions to guide your opening remarks:

1. What's the team's purpose?
2. What's the context? How did we get to this point? What's our history with other, similar teams?
3. Why are you on this team? What criteria did I/we use in selecting this group?
4. What tools or resources do you need?
5. How will I/we measure your success?

Answering these questions up front signals to the group that you've thought through its purpose and mapped out its strategy. You'll also show that even though you're new to the job, you intend to hold the team accountable for achieving certain results.

You probably know what it's like to get picked to serve on a team. If you were already busy trying to rush through your own job duties, you may have viewed your team assignment as an annoying, time-wasting burden.

But if the team leader assured you that you were chosen for a specific reason—your expertise or experience, perhaps—and explained succinctly how the team could reshape the organization's future, your initial cynicism probably melted away. That's why your ability to lead teams is really a test of your communication skills.

SMART MANAGING

POP QUIZ

Here's an exercise to determine if you've effectively communicated to team members why the team exists. Approach a sampling of team members in private. Ask each of them the same question: *How would you describe the team's purpose?* Ideally, everyone should give you the same answer with little or no hesitation.

Informing members about the team's goals and mission may seem like a no-brainer. But sloppy or disorganized managers often skip this crucial step.

Ineffectual managers might also form teams for the wrong reasons. Examples of misguided motives to assemble a team include:

- As window dressing to disguise behind-the-scenes moves that employees will resent
- To develop and evaluate options when you've already made up your mind
- To handle "drudge work" that individuals left on their own fail to do
- To indulge a senior executive, board member, or other VIP who urges you to create a team (even though you don't agree a team is necessary)
- To deflect attention from your own dithering, because the team must make decisions that you're reluctant to make

Figure out the best way to pinpoint the team's purpose and articulate it with clarity. This preparatory process forces you to confront your core aim in forming the group—and to uncover groundless or mistaken reasons that can lead you astray. The sooner you acknowledge and address these judgment errors, the better.

Give Everyone Equal Attention

Rookie managers often fall into the trap of allowing the most vocal individuals to dominate team meetings. Outspoken, take-charge types can energize a group. But they can also squelch debate and leave shy folks retreating into the shadows.

Letting extroverts hog the floor comes with many risks. They might derail the collaborative spirit you want to instill in the group. And their comments can divert people from higher-priority issues—or spark needless controversy when you'd rather prevent distractions and keep everyone focused on the critical work ahead.

You also need to craft an image as a fair-minded manager who values everyone's input. That means more than telling a motormouth to wrap up and let others contribute. You also want to make eye contact with each individual, even the quietest, easy-to-overlook members. When someone interrupts a diffident speaker in midsentence, step in and say, "Please ignore that interruption and go on." Once you let one person interrupt and get away with it, you set a bad precedent that will stymie subsequent team discussions.

As you gain management experience, you will learn how to lavish equal attention on everyone in the room. For now, your challenge is to silence the chronic talkers so that others can make their voices heard.

Here are three techniques to help you hear from even the most bashful wallflowers within your team:

1. **Go one by one.** Participants take turns based on seating order. This way, every member gets a turn to speak. But beware: going around the room can waste time if people merely repeat what's already been said.
2. **Hands up.** Ask people who wish to speak to raise their hands. Then recognize each speaker. Eventually, you may want to turn to those who haven't raised their hands and prompt them to share their thoughts.
3. **Pass the baton.** A member speaks only when he or she possesses a prop such as a baton. When speakers finish, they hand the prop to someone else who requests it. This method works best when you have a potentially unruly group of fiery, high-energy personalities.

IN PRAISE OF INTROVERTS

In her influential book, *Quiet: The Power of Introverts in a World That Can't Stop Talking*, author Susan Cain writes, "There's zero correlation between being the best talker and having the best ideas." She

TOOLS cautions managers that in order to maximize everyone's contribution, avoid holding a meeting, sitting back, and letting the ideas flow. This will only enable the most vocally assertive individuals to dominate. Instead, she suggests requesting that everyone submit ideas or opinions in writing before the meeting. Then use the written replies to trigger a more inclusive discussion where everyone gets a chance to speak.

The more you know your team, the more you can facilitate discussions by bringing in diverse voices. If the conversation shifts to a technical topic, you might turn to a shy technician and say, "This is right up your alley, given your specialized know-how. What do you think?"

Another way to spread participation to everyone on the team—from quiet clams to merry jokesters—involves role-plays. Assign pairs of employees to act out a simple scenario that's related to the team's mission. Then extract learning points from their "performance."

To generate ideas to improve customer service, for example, make sure everyone gets to play a role as either a client or a service rep. This gets every team member front and center—and makes it tough for anyone to hide in the back of the room.

Finally, keep circulating among your group. Move closer to quieter individuals and make supportive gestures and eye contact with them to indicate that you want them to speak up. If you stay planted at one end of a long conference table the whole time, you may wind up focusing on the same two or three faces and ignore everyone seated farther away.

Confront Conflict Head-On

What's the worst piece of advice given to new managers? My vote goes to, "Avoid conflict at all cost."

You cannot escape on-the-job conflict. Now that you're a manager, you'll get roped into more rancorous situations than you ever thought possible.

Managing teams and managing conflict go hand in hand. Many individuals chafe at the notion of collaborating with peers whom they don't like or don't trust. Some teams wage internecine wars over who gets credit or who's to blame. In other cases, petty squabbles erupt over perceived slights or cliques that form within groups.

While it's easier to manage harmonious teams, don't get too discouraged if you find yourself immersed in a conflict-ridden group of malcontents. Research shows that well-managed conflict can work to the group's advantage in its pursuit of shared objectives. The conflict can even prod members to devise more creative solutions as bluntness and boldness drive better results.

CLASSIFY THE CONFLICT

As soon as you detect conflict within a team, analyze whether it revolves around the work itself or the personalities involved. Ask yourself, "Are people arguing over *how* or *why* certain tasks need to be done—or picking fights that aren't related to the job at hand?" If they're battling over strategy or execution, that's not necessarily a bad sign. Such a conflict can lift everyone's performance. But if they're embroiled in personality clashes, you're better off intervening.

You have a choice as manager: you can ignore brewing conflicts and wait for them to blow over. Or you can step in and demand that people find a way to work together.

The passive approach rarely works, at least in the long term. Conflicts may eventually de-escalate or die out on their own, but they leave lasting scars. Ill will lingers. Resentments fester. People take sides.

Intervening makes more sense, but it's often stressful to insert yourself into the fray. The last thing you want is to play referee, proclaiming a "winner" and "loser" like in a boxing match.

Yet conflict, like cancer, tends to spread. When it infiltrates a team, a spillover effect typically occurs: the group's anger can prove so debilitating that it undermines workers' productivity in all aspects of their job. That's why you need to contain team turmoil as soon as it flares up.

In some cases, you won't be able to contain team conflict. As much as you try to listen respectfully to all sides and urge key players to reach a resolution, you may find the issues or personalities are intractable.

Rather than belabor the matter, change the subject. Say, "It appears we cannot solve this right now, so let's jump to the next agenda item."

TIME FOR A SIS!

To redirect warring team members toward a productive goal, jolt them out of their antagonistic status quo. How? Stage a "SIS" meeting (Short, Informal, Spontaneous). Gather the team (or just **TOOLS** those aggrieved members who are dragging down the rest of the group) on a moment's notice. Present them with an impending dilemma that merits their full attention. Perhaps a regulatory agency just notified you that its representatives will make a surprise visit tomorrow and you need your team to prepare. Mobilizing everyone to conquer a crisis can induce combatants to set aside their differences for the greater good.

Assure the group that you'll support any efforts to resolve the conflict, but time is of the essence. Asserting your authority in this manner will boost your credibility in your new role.

Your job is to lead a team to meet its goals, not solve its problems. You cannot dish out solutions like dollar bills as a kind of well-meaning prize. But you can listen to all sides, show interest in everyone's point of view, and redirect the group's energy to maximize its impact.

The Truth About Brainstorming

You can't lose by brainstorming great ideas with your team, right? Gathering a group and letting everyone chime in seems like a surefire winner, right?

Actually, there's a right and wrong way to brainstorm. And sometimes, it's better to avoid it entirely if you want to generate the boldest ideas from the widest possible swath of employees.

When Alex Osborn, an advertising executive, popularized the concept of brainstorming in the 1940s, he sought a method to solve problems. He wanted to pool the best ideas from groups and, through free-flowing information sharing, enable individuals to fuel each other's creativity.

For Osborn, brainstorming at its best featured certain characteristics. Groups could speak freely without fear of criticism from peers or managers ("There are no dumb ideas"). They could veer from the narrow confines of the subject matter to suggest more outlandish proposals ("Let your minds run wild"). Quantity comes before quality ("I want at least 10 ideas from each of you").

For about 40 years, brain-storming took off. Pricey consultants taught managers how to facilitate these sessions and drive teams to new levels of ideation.

> **Ideation** A dynamic, creative process for developing new ideas, often through team meetings or exercises.
>
>
>
> **KEY TERM**

Since the early 1990s, however, researchers have questioned some of the perceived benefits of brainstorming. Susan Cain champions solitude as a prerequisite for creative breakthroughs, especially for introverts who thrive when given the chance to function in uninterrupted privacy.

In a widely read *New Yorker* article in 2012, Jonah Lehrer reviewed much of the latest academic thinking and concluded that brainstorming doesn't work. He suggested that managers in search of innovative insights abandon group meetings and, instead, allow individuals to concentrate on their own theories and potential break-throughs. Managers can collect their employees' ideas in writing and, mixing and matching particularly promising strains of each person's output, pool the collective wisdom of their workforce.

> **TOO MUCH ACCEPTANCE**
>
> **CAUTION**
>
> It sounds enlightened to assure brainstorming employees, "No idea is stupid." But in fact, some ideas are stupid. Put more charitably, they're unworkable or unrealistic. Recent research indicates that criticizing such dubious contributions from employees actually stokes team creativity. As long as you're polite and respectful, it's fine to say, "We need lower-cost solutions" or "We lack the resources to implement anything on that scale."

In their eagerness to curry favor with employees, new managers sometimes facilitate brainstorming sessions that lapse into everyone's-a-genius gushing. Complimenting everything that comes out of your staffers' mouths will not endear you to them; in fact, they'll soon suspect that you lack judgment.

One of the most disingenuous ways to respond to a glaringly bad idea is to say earnestly with a straight face, "That's interesting. Let's expand on that and see where it leads us." But it's far better to say, "Let's shift our focus a bit." Then pose a question such as, "What are some simpler ways to harness our strengths?" or "How about some low-cost alternatives?"

To save yourself—and your team—from fruitless hours of unproductive meetings, start by posing a challenge to the group in the form of a simple question. Examples include, "How can we increase customer retention?" or "What are we overlooking in terms of protecting our data from cyberattacks?"

Then ask each staffer to submit to you at least one specific action step in writing. Use the responses as a springboard for debate, either in person or via online exchange.

Old-fashioned brainstorming can play an important but limited role. Just don't make it your default strategy for generating great ideas from teams.

Know What You Don't Know

New managers sometimes assume the key to effective team meetings is giving a stirring opening speech and then motivating everyone to care about a successful outcome. But you're not a football coach pumping up your players before a big game.

Even if you pose an exciting challenge to the group and make every member feel important and driven to win, the ensuing conversation can prove disappointing. Participants may jockey for prominence on the team and advocate for their narrow viewpoint. Instead of collaborating for the greater good, they can expend too much energy seeking credit for their contribution.

There's a better way to get the most out of teams and arrive at the wisest, most informed decisions. If your goal is to facilitate a discussion about a specific issue, start by presenting your opinion. Say, "Here's how I see the situation. To what extent do you see it differently?"

After you lay out your understanding of the matter at hand, show interest in learning from the team. Urge the group to help you get a better sense of the issue. Highlight the range of expertise and experience in the room—and praise team members' know-how as it relates to the topic.

As participants share their ideas and input, don't rush to judge what you hear. First, summarize the message and ask, "Have I got that right?" By paraphrasing what you hear and allowing employees to confirm that you accurately captured their point, you implicitly signal that you're listening raptly.

ASSERTIVE INQUIRY

At Procter & Gamble, the global consumer goods company, CEO A. G. Lafley embraces what he calls "assertive inquiry" to guide teams. His goal is to lead them to move beyond advocating for their own view so that they're more open to teammates' views. To do this, he coaches employees to state their case while adopting the attitude, "I have a view worth hearing, but I may be missing something." This sets the stage for more give-and-take as peers learn from each other rather than insist their view or proposal is the "right" one.

FOR EXAMPLE

Finally, dig to learn more. Fill any gaps in your interpretation of the team's views. Examples include asking, "So what other repercussions do you see if we close our branch office?" or "How much are you willing to sacrifice short-term revenue for longer-term relationship building?"

Teams appreciate the chance to dive deeply into issues. Test their analytic skills by posing rigorous questions that trigger more sophisticated debate.

Model how you want others to behave. Present your opinions as provisional—as subject to change—and welcome spirited debate. Let team discussions flow without jumping in to correct every misstatement or "fix" someone who takes a contrarian stance. Allowing others to express wide-ranging opinions without instantly judging them paves the way for real collaboration in a trustful environment.

Expect some rocky roads along the way. Running teams rarely comes easily, even to experienced managers. Whenever you gather diverse personalities and rally them to collaborate, diversions and digressions can stymie their progress.

Richard Hackman, a Harvard University psychology professor who died in 2013 after decades of researching teams, wrote, "Although my main aspiration has been to provide guidance that will be useful to team leaders and members, there are no 'one-minute' prescriptions—creating, leading, and serving on teams is not that simple."

In a 2011 *Harvard Business Review* article, Hackman listed some misconceptions about teamwork. As a new manager, you might be relieved to learn that one of the misconceptions involves the nature of team leadership. Hackman challenged the common view that "it all depends on the leader."

Instead, he argued that effective leaders do three things well: create conditions for participants to thrive on their own, launch teams in the right direction, and provide hands-on coaching along the way. Team leaders thus play a critical role, but it's more supportive than dominant.

Part of the challenge in creating the right conditions for teams is recruiting the right people to participate. Resist the urge to pad teams with extraneous members. Bigger does not mean better. When you ask more than 10 people to serve on a committee or collaborate on a clearly defined task, odds are at least a few of those people will give minimal effort, keep quiet, and evade responsibility. On a small team, it's harder to hide. To achieve collective success, everyone has to step up and play a vital role.

PICK THE RIGHT SIZE

TOOLS

When forming teams, only recruit individuals who bring definable strengths or competencies to the group. Don't add people who cannot add value—or you risk assembling a flabby, overly large team. Max Ringelmann, a French agricultural engineer, wrote in 1913 that the more people who pull on a rope, the less effort each puller exerts. So pick each member with care to ensure he or she brings distinct skills, technical prowess, or other irreplaceable talents that the team needs.

Keeping teams small, with well-chosen members who each bring unique skills and perspectives, sets the stage for fast-moving progress. But don't stop there. Engage teams in the process of discovery and experimentation. Admit that you don't have all the answers, and that's why you are looking to the group for its collective insight.

When teams report their findings to you, respond with openness and curiosity. Ask lots of follow-up questions such as:

- How did you arrive at that conclusion?
- How would you describe the level of debate or disagreement over this issue?
- Can you elaborate on your recommendations? (Pros and cons, risks and rewards, etc.?)
- In your research, what facts, figures, or other data surprised you the most?
- What did you learn through the course of your work together?

Showering the team with questions shows that you take their work seriously and you're eager to learn. Some new managers mistakenly assume they must react to a team's findings by nodding and saying, "Yep, that's right. You reinforced what I already know." In fact, managers who readily acknowledge what they don't know—and who express genuine interest in filling in the gaps—tend to extract the most insight from groups.

Better yet, you motivate people when you dignify their knowledge. Allowing them to educate you may strike you as a humble gesture. But it's more than that. By peppering teams with questions and digesting the answers with an open mind, you position yourself to make smarter, more informed decisions. Groups realize that they really serve a purpose—and that you intend to listen and learn.

In Chapter 6, you learned that the top motivator for many people is advancing on meaningful projects. When employees make progress on assignments that they deem meaningful to the organization, they derive more satisfaction from their job. When you guide your team to pursue exciting goals—and you invest the time and curiosity to learn from the group's efforts—everyone comes away smarter and more motivated to succeed.

New Manager's Checklist for Chapter 13

☑ Define the team's purpose. Reinforce that message so that everyone knows why you formed the team and what it's supposed to accomplish.

☑ When leading team meetings, treat everyone equally. Ensure all participants get a chance to speak. Don't let loudmouths dominate the proceedings.

☑ As soon as you detect conflict within a team, analyze the source of the conflict and determine whether you need to intervene. Don't assume it'll go away on its own.

☑ Team brainstorming has a limited but sometimes useful role. Facilitate idea-sharing sessions in a focused, disciplined manner and be honest if people make inane or unhelpful contributions.

☑ Weigh the benefits of forgoing brainstorming meetings in favor of asking individuals to submit their best ideas in writing.

☑ Let teams help you learn. Start by stating your opinion on a key issue and then asking for input and inviting differing views.

☑ After you lay out your understanding of the matter at hand, be willing to let team members change your mind or broaden your perspective.

☑ When teams present their findings or recommendations, ask follow-up questions. Dig to learn more and find out how they arrived at their conclusions.

Five Tests Every Manager Faces

I magine we could transport a manager from 1950 into today's work-place. Would that person recognize what it's like to supervise people in the twenty-first century?

Aside from the most visible changes—different clothing styles and everyone fiddling with handheld electronic gadgets (and no smoking!)—the basics remain the same. Managers still need to maximize the performance of their employees.

Yet today's supervisors face challenges distinct from past generations. Here are five of the most important tests that new managers must pass to succeed amid an ever-changing economic and cultural backdrop:

1. **Managing contract workers.** As more organizations enlist individuals to tackle short-term projects, plug personnel holes on a temporary basis, or handle technical tasks, managers must get the most out of nonemployees. These people lack allegiance to your employer. *How do you motivate them to excel and embrace your culture—when they're outsiders?*

2. **Supervising off-site workers.** A decade ago, a handful of forward-looking employers let some people work from home. Today, it's common for managers to oversee far-flung staffers who may go months or years without meeting face-to-face. *If you cannot see them every day, how do you know they're doing the work?*

3. **Managing peers.** Traditionally, supervisors were put in charge of subordinates—underlings at a lower rung of the ladder. As the old-fashioned organizational hierarchy gets flattened like a pancake, managers increasingly find themselves managing peers. *If you're working alongside coworkers some of the time—but now you're also in charge of supervising them—how can you wear both hats?*

4. **Spying on workers.** If our 1950 manager wanted to spy on an employee, it would involve lurking in the shadows and surreptitiously taking notes like a private detective. Today, managers can use technological tools that are far more intrusive. *To what extent should you use surveillance technologies to monitor workers' web use and other behaviors?*

5. **Combating workplace violence.** While the incidence of such violence isn't soaring (despite frantic media coverage), the severity of such events continues to instill fear. *What steps can you take to recognize the warning signs and address the threat of potentially violent individuals at work?*

To pass each of these tests, you'll need to rethink your role. Sixty years ago, a boss could bark orders and demand compliance—or else. It's not that simple today. There are nuances that new managers must master, from observing an employee's nonverbal cues more closely to listening more attentively.

The tests that you need to pass to succeed in management require a wide range of skills. You must develop keen ethical judgment in an era when ethics are hotly debated but muddier than ever. You need to embrace technological advances that at first glance may strike you as

---

COMPUTERS AT WORK

FOR EXAMPLE

The challenges that today's new managers face are shaped by technology. As management expert Peter Drucker wrote in *Management Challenges for the 21st Century* (HarperCollins, 1999), "A half century ago, around 1950, prevailing opinion overwhelmingly held that the market for that new 'miracle,' the computer, would be in the military and in scientific calculations, for example, astronomy." As it turns out, computing applications have revolutionized almost every aspect of managing people—from tracking the whereabouts of mobile workers to measuring their productivity.

impersonal tools that distance you from your staff. And you can expect to face complex communication challenges such as conveying clear, multi-step instructions to diverse types of workers who each reside in separate locations.

Through all these changes, remember that you're not infallible. Admitting what you don't know—and seeking answers from those who do—is one of the hallmarks of top-performing new managers.

Managing Contract Workers

Managers, both rookies and grizzled veterans, often assume that contract workers cannot possibly bring the same level of commitment as full-time employees. They may equate outsiders as mercenaries who parachute into the organization, contribute their narrow expertise, and move on without any emotional investment in their work.

Yet ask contractors how *they* feel and you'll get an earful. Many of them crave a sense of belonging. When they get hired on a per-project basis, they may care just as much about producing quality work—and leaving a lasting positive impression—as your most driven, reliable full-timers.

Strive to get acquainted with contractors before their first day on the job. This gives you a chance to learn about their professional background and find out what motivates them. A 10-minute chat can help you bond with them and adjust your management style to accommodate their needs and maximize the results.

When vetting a contractor, ask yourself three questions:

1. Have I defined the assignment with precision (including time frames for completion and metrics that will determine success)?

INTRODUCE NEWCOMERS TO OLD-TIMERS

SMART

MANAGING

A contractor who suddenly shows up at work may leave your employees in a tizzy. They may wonder about this person's role, scope of duties, and background. To increase the odds of instant camaraderie, introduce contract workers to your workforce in a forthright manner. Anticipate and address employees' questions in an e-mail to your team that includes a few personal tidbits about the contractor, his or her job objectives, and a description of any specific projects that the individual will tackle.

2. To what extent can the contractor's relationship evolve with the organization? (i.e., is there an opportunity over the long term to get hired full-time?)

3. How can I ensure that the contractor embraces, or at least accepts, our culture?

The final question is perhaps the toughest to answer. It's hard enough to ensure that permanent employees fit comfortably into your culture. Trying to assess whether an outsider whom you barely know possesses the character and personality to thrive in your workplace can require a leap of faith. What's worse, you may not interview contractors with the same rigor that you apply to selecting full-time candidates.

Consider how your staff will view the contract worker. You want to create an environment where the two parties get along and know each other's roles and authority levels. That may mean laying out the business case for bringing in the contractor (cost savings, contribute hard-to-find expertise, etc.) and dangling incentives for teams to integrate the outsider seamlessly to attain the goals you've set.

Stephan Furnari, founder of Law Firm Suites, often hires contract workers for his New York firm that provides office space to attorneys. He told Forbes.com that he needs to be "painstakingly detailed with the instructions I give because [contractors] don't have the luxury to learn by being around the office." By laying out specific instructions, connecting contract workers to relevant tools and resources within your organization, and maintaining ongoing contact with them, you help them hit the ground running.

When managing contractors, conflicts can erupt over how they spend their time. For example, they may search for new clients while ostensibly working for you.

HAPPY CAMPERS?

CAUTION Some contract workers operate not by choice, but by necessity: they were laid off from their full-time job and need to generate income. And they may not be happy about it. Probe to determine a contractor's attitude. Don't focus solely on the individual's technical qualifications; ask questions such as, "What led you to become a contractor?" so that you can assess their eagerness to cooperate with employees and function as part of a team.

Set productivity goals for outsiders so that they know what you expect—and how you'll evaluate them. It's easier to show flexibility (say, if they make personal calls on company time) if you've defined what constitutes acceptable performance.

Supervising People You Can't See

Managing people who work from home—or other remote locations—is a balancing act. On one hand, you might assume these independent-minded folks just want to be left alone to do their job. They strike you as disciplined self-starters who don't need much hand-holding.

On the other hand, you realize you cannot afford to ignore them or take them for granted. They may enjoy working on their own, free from office chitchat and swirling distractions. But that doesn't mean they want to be cast adrift entirely, excluded from the community built around you and the rest of your team.

For new managers trying to assert their leadership over a far-flung workforce, supervising people from afar revolves around trust. Can you trust someone you can't see daily?

If you're controlling by nature, your anxiety may rise when your calls or e-mails go unreturned for an hour or two. It's tempting to think, "This person is goofing off. What's going on over there?"

To build trust, start by setting clear production standards. When employees know what you expect in terms of quantifiable output and quality measures, they will understand your criteria for evaluating them. That in itself will foster a stronger working relationship.

At least once a week, benchmark the individual's performance against your standards. In a call or e-mail, praise the off-site worker for exceeding expectations or express concern if you see indications of underperformance. Ongoing communication signals your engagement in the employee—and your interest in supporting that person's success.

Harness technology to your advantage. Off-site employees often rely on social media and other online tools to forge connections with co-workers. In Chapter 6, we discussed how an organization can develop a "wiki"—an internal web platform—to motivate a workforce that's scattered around the world. Intranets and in-house "wikis" also bring

TRICKS
OF THE
TRADE

HERE'S YOUR DAILY CALL

To ensure ongoing communication with off-site employees, use recording software to broadcast your comments far and wide. An increasing number of CEOs and business owners make daily recordings—often under two minutes—that workers around the world can hear via the phone or online audio download. Use your recorded message to share the latest news about your team and the organization as a whole. Update listeners on procedural changes, customer input, or ways to improve performance. Hearing your voice for just a minute or two a day—and knowing that all their colleagues are receiving the same message—can make remote workers feel more connected to you and more informed about their employer.

together virtual teams. When individuals housed thousands of miles apart can log in and share experiences and exchange information, they get a chance to collaborate and regain at least some of the benefits they're missing by working from separate locations.

One of the toughest challenges in supervising off-site employees is making up for what you miss. When you walk down the hall six times a day and see your staffer, you can instantly sense that person's energy level and commitment. You can't do that from across the country, although videoconferencing can give you limited opportunities to communicate face-to-face.

Customize your management style to offset the downside of supervising from a distance. Ravi Gajendran, a professor of business administration at the University of Illinois at Urbana-Champaign, suggests that managers use what he calls a "leader-member exchange" approach to supervise remote staff. This means developing a more personal relationship with each off-site employee that involves listening, showing interest, and giving and receiving feedback in an easygoing, supportive manner.

Through his research, Gajendran has found that virtual workers sometimes feel like their contributions aren't appreciated or even acknowledged. A sense of isolation can set it, leaving these individuals disengaged and disgruntled.

Don't let your far-off workers feel invisible! Serve as their internal champion, promoting their efforts in companywide newsletters, e-mail blasts, and congratulatory rewards. Advocate for their career advancement and professional development. Arrange for them to meet VIPs such as the CEO or tour an influential customer's facility.

Because virtual employees rely so heavily on information technology, review your organization's policies relating to confidentiality and data security. Researchers are finding that at-home workers don't necessarily stay at home. They may plant themselves at multiple locations ranging from a café to a library to a park bench. Huddle with your technology managers to identify potential security risks at alternate sites and craft written policies to safeguard data as well as your employees.

SECURE YOUR DATA

With the explosion in cyberattacks and data breaches, organizations are taking more steps to protect their proprietary information (from customers' credit card numbers to new-product prototypes). Managing distant workers thus requires managing the secure sharing of data files. Train your team to take precautions with internal data, especially if they're engaged in the confidential exchange of protected health, financial, or administrative information.

Managing Peers

When you're promoted into people management, you want to develop a respectful relationship with your staff. But that's tricky if you're doubling as their supervisor while still doing the grunt work alongside them.

In flat organizations, fewer tiers of management often leave newly minted supervisors retaining at least some duties from their old job. That's especially true with hard-to-replace technical experts; they may find themselves supervising other technicians—their peers—even as they continue to devote part of their workday to the nonmanagerial tasks that they've performed for years.

Assuming you're not the power-hungry, bossy type, you may find managing peers a source of great discomfort. Disciplining employees, administering performance reviews, and prodding laggards to deliver better results require take-charge leadership. It's one thing to lead subordinates who operate well below your pay grade, but it's awkward to direct people who are essentially your equals.

The way in which you step into your new role can influence how your peers perceive you. Hopefully, a human resources officer or senior executive will alert everyone of your promotion. But don't sit passively on the sidelines and let others stage the transition. You'll want to help send the right message. Make sure the memo specifies when the changeover will occur, the scope of your new responsibilities, and who will field questions about your role (presumably an HR rep).

FRIENDS FOREVER? NOT REALLY ...

CAUTION

You know all those friendships you enjoy with your colleagues? Those days are over. As the new boss, you must recalibrate those relationships. That means less socializing during or after work. Otherwise, you'll be vulnerable to accusations of favoritism. Tell your peers, "As much as I respect you and like spending time with you, my new position requires that I introduce a little bit more distance."

This may all seem obvious. But in many organizations, new managers step into their position in a vacuum. Anxious and confused, employees might spread rumors about the rationale for the changes or the basis for your promotion. Such gossip can prove distracting and undermine morale at a particularly critical time.

One of the advantages of supervising peers is that you can probably gather frank feedback from them. Welcome that input—the more, the better. Urge the most trusted members of your team to tell you how you're doing on a regular basis.

Don't wait for them to volunteer. In a private moment, ask, "How can I improve as a manager?" and "Can you share any observations related to my performance?"

When you must do your old job—whether it's an auditor or engineer—wear only that hat. If coworkers demand a pay raise or complain about working conditions, say, "I hear you. But right now, I'm concentrating on getting this job done. Can we discuss this issue tomorrow when I can focus on it better?"

Throughout this book, you've learned that new managers should not pretend to know everything. When you're dealing with peers, look for opportunities to say, "I don't have all the answers. What do you think?" Then publicly credit them for their contributions in helping you manage,

YOUR OPINION COUNTS

FOR EXAMPLE

Amy Gallo, a contributing editor at *Harvard Business Review*, wrote about Rusty O'Kelley, a partner in a consulting firm. After O'Kelley was chosen by his peers to become managing partner, he met one-on-one with each member of his team—42 people—and sought their input. Then he convened a group meeting to share what he learned and set goals for the year. He even announced how he was improving internal processes thanks to ideas from his peers. "I wanted to signal that I cared about everyone's opinions," he said.

especially when you're meeting with top executives or other key influencers both inside and outside your organization.

When you become a manager, don't assume your peers will treat you the same way as before—or communicate with you as they once did. Instead, expect a wide range of behavioral changes. Resentful workers (perhaps they're jealous or angry they lost out on the promotion) might cast you as an adversary, avoiding eye contact and shutting down when you try to engage them. Formerly friendly coworkers may shun you because they tend to view all managers as tainted or worthy of scorn. And formerly aloof colleagues may suddenly shower you with kindness in an effort to advance their own ambitions and curry favor with you.

Spying on Workers

Over the last decade, annual surveys of American employers show that electronic surveillance of employees increases every year. This can include monitoring e-mail and Internet use as well as the proliferation of video cameras at work.

The surge in interest in employee monitoring does not mean you should hop on the bandwagon and start spying tomorrow. The need varies based on many factors, ranging from the nature of the work that people do at your organization to the culture within which everyone operates.

Today's new managers function in a working world where social media and technological trends take center stage. Workplace privacy protections, once a quaint back-burner issue, now preoccupy attorneys, HR managers, and employees at all levels.

KEY TERM **Keylogging** Recording the keys that someone hits on a keyboard, often logged in secret so that the user doesn't know that his or her keystrokes are being monitored.

On-the-go field employees are getting pulled into the debate. While the legality of using Global Positioning Systems (GPS) is always changing, some employers can use GPS trackers to follow drivers (in both company-owned and even employee-owned vehicles).

Surveillance software keeps getting more sophisticated. Products can record every keystroke, e-mail, and instant message that someone types on a keyboard. A manager can arrange to receive a log file (which lists all such activity) and review it regularly.

Many managers rave about these technologies, which make spying easy. There are countless stories of supervisors using electronic surveillance to discover an employee viewing online pornography at work or wasting big chunks of the day downloading recipes, revealing proprietary data to unauthorized individuals, or hunting for jobs.

Research your employer's electronic surveillance policies. What tools and resources are available to managers? When—and how—can you use them? Make sure you understand the legal ramifications of employee monitoring in all its forms, from eavesdropping on their phone calls to checking their voice mail and their sent and received e-mails.

In many organizations, spying occurs on an as-needed basis. An employee's questionable behavior triggers an investigation, and that in turn leads to the retrieval and review of electronic surveillance records.

After you document your suspicion that an employee might be violating the law or an organizational policy, focused surveillance can kick in. Make sure to get written consent from your human resources team and your organization's attorney before you proceed.

Communicating your organization's surveillance policies in plain English to all employees helps spread awareness and reduce your legal liability. As a general rule, alert your workforce of the steps you—and other managers—can take to monitor their activities.

In your first few weeks on the job, get a feel for how more experienced managers at your organization treat electronic surveillance. Probe to find

---

SPYING IN ALL DIRECTIONS

In 2012, an employee at a Christian publishing firm secretly taped the CEO in a testy internal meeting. Angry at staffers for bad-mouthing the company, the CEO fired 25 employees on the spot. He had unearthed their critical comments about the firm by monitoring their digital activities. According to Forbes.com, the CEO ranted, "I got to read some of your Facebook pages. My favorite is when you post something and then take it down and don't think we archive it all."

---

out how they balance the need to show trust in people versus the temptation to harness monitoring software and other technologies to ensure rule compliance and measure productivity.

If you're ethically queasy about spying on employees, get over it. New managers often find such monitoring distasteful. But the more you notice workers hiding their screens when you're nearby (or spending long hours typing away while their output and work product mysteriously declines), the more you'll come around. Surveys indicate that more than 60 percent of American employers engage in various forms of electronic surveillance, so you're not the only snooping manager out there.

Combating Workplace Violence

Comb the research on workplace violence, and you wind up a confused mess. The number of homicides at work is dropping. But nonfatal incidents are increasing. No, they're decreasing. But wait: some experts claim that violent acts are underreported at work.

Your risk of experiencing violence at work is probably low. A 2013 study published in *Aggression and Violent Behavior* found that such violence is rare and the risk "varies by demographic factors and occupational status (and in some cases their interaction, such as female nurses) as well as by the nature of the victim-aggressor relationship—with most workplace violence originating from persons external to the workplace."

Every so often, a high-profile workplace shooting or other heavily reported event captures our interest. Anxiety spreads. People return to work and see new security measures in place such as more guards, cameras, and metal detectors.

You're a new manager, not a superhero. No one's expecting you to ward off violent criminals. But it pays to know the warning signs of possible brewing violence—and what to do if you spot these red flags.

In your first few months as a manager, observe your staff closely along with key outsiders who interact regularly with your team. Identify their baseline behaviors. Notice their normal rate of speech, facial expressions, and body language. Watch how they walk and how they use their hands when they talk. Pay special attention to abrupt changes in their demeanor—and what triggers may account for those changes.

All these observations serve a purpose. By understanding how someone behaves under normal circumstances, you're more apt to detect when that person acts inconsistently. Veering from one's baseline behavior in alarming ways can indicate a potential for violence.

CREATE A CHECKLIST

Draft a "cheat sheet" to help you spot potentially violent individuals. List some warning signs and refer to them when you want to conduct a quick threat assessment. Examples of what to look

TOOLS   for in others: exhibits stress, refuses to accept any blame or admit any fault, looks uncharacteristically disheveled, starts breaking rules or ignoring safety procedures, discusses weapons with intensifying interest, misses work without adequate explanation, picks verbal fights with coworkers, behaves erratically, and undergoes wild mood swings.

The most common workplace violence occurs when someone with minimal or no ties to your organization commits a criminal act such as a robbery. In that case, there's little you can do ahead of time.

Other instances of violence can involve disturbed customers, individuals who work for other employers in the same building, or familiar outsiders who frequently visit your facility. Sometimes, employees come to blows with each other. And then there's the scourge of domestic violence, which can infiltrate your workplace in the form of a worker's current or former partner.

Hopefully, your employer provides training to help you—and everyone else on the premises—identify and report threats. The most enlightened organizations also develop a workplace violence prevention policy built around "zero tolerance" for any type of threat.

Supported by a comprehensive written policy, you can pounce on any infraction. If an employee issues a menacing verbal threat, for instance, you know to document the incident and notify your HR manager.

Here's where managing people can cause sleepless nights. Once you set disciplinary steps in motion, the employee who made a verbal threat might turn all sweet and innocent and say, "Oh, come on! I was joking." Doubts creep in. You wonder if you're overreacting.

Here's some final advice to help you succeed (and stay sane) as a manager: Stick to your principles. Act consistently. If there's a clearly stated rule in your workplace and someone violates it, then play the enforcer—100 percent of the time.

There will be opportunities to debate the merits of the rule later. Maybe it needs to soften based on changing circumstances. But for now, it's there in black and white— written and distributed to employees as an unambiguous policy for all to follow.

Your employees may not like you for enforcing the rules. But they will respect you. And that's the kind of invaluable currency that will help you thrive as a manager and a leader.

New Manager's Checklist for Chapter 14

☑ When hiring contract workers, define the assignment clearly and assess to what extent they're aligned with your organizational culture.

☑ Set productivity goals for contractors and off-site employees to avoid any confusion about what you expect and how you'll evaluate them.

☑ Communicate regularly with a far-flung workforce by recording calls to your team and checking in one-on-one by phone and e-mail.

☑ Look for opportunities to advocate for your off-site workers. Help them gain visibility among senior executives at your organization, and publicize their contributions internally.

☑ Seek frequent feedback from the peers you supervise, but don't try to maintain friendships with them.

☑ Engage in electronic surveillance of employees when you suspect possible violation of the law or an internal policy, rather than spy on them without cause.

☑ Create a list of warning signs of workplace violence, and use it to assess potential threats.

☑ Enforce rules consistently when in comes to maintaining a safe, respectful work environment.

Index

Index

About the Author

Morey Stettner is a writer and communication skills coach in Portsmouth, New Hampshire. He's the author of *The Art of Winning Conversation* (Prentice Hall), which shows you how to listen and win over others in your personal and professional life, and *The Manager's Survival Guide* (McGraw-Hill). He's editor of *Executive Leadership*, a monthly newsletter published by Business Management Daily in McLean, Virginia. He also writes weekly articles on leadership for *Investor's Business Daily*. A dynamic speaker and seminar leader, he has led hundreds of training programs across the United States on topics such as sales skills, public speaking, and attentive listening. He graduated *magna cum laude* from Brown University. You can e-mail him at m.stettner@comcast.net.